101 J254

P9-AFZ-347

SHAKER ▴ STYLE

SHAKER·STYLE

THE GIFT OF SIMPLICITY

CANDACE ORD MANROE
WITH JOSEPH BOEHM

CRESCENT BOOKS
New York

A FRIEDMAN GROUP BOOK

This 1991 edition published by Crescent Books, distributed by Outlet Book Company, Inc., a Random House Company, 225 Park Avenue South, New York, New York 10003.

Copyright © 1991 by Michael Friedman Publishing Group, Inc.

All rights reserved. No part of this publication may be reproduced, stored in a retrieval system, or transmitted, in any form or by any means, electronic, photocopying, recording, or otherwise, without the prior written permission of the publisher.

ISBN 0-517-02009-2

SHAKER STYLE:
The Gift of Simplicity
was prepared and produced by
Michael Friedman Publishing Group, Inc.
15 West 26th Street
New York, New York 10010

Editor: Sharon Kalman
Art Director: Jeff Batzli
Designer: Lynne Yeamans
Layout: Helayne Messing
Photography Editor: Daniella Jo Nilva
Illustrations by Judy L. Morgan

Additional photo credits: p. 19, © Brian Vanden Brink/Sabbathday Lake, ME; p. 28, © George Goodwin/Mount Lebanon, NY; p. 45, © George Goodwin/Mount Lebanon, NY; p. 79 © Jeanetta Ho/Dunham Tavern Museum Collection; p. 98, © Mary Nemeth/ Pleasant Hill, KY; p. 101, © Philip M. Zito/Dunham Tavern Museum Collection; p. 117, © Jeff Greenberg/ Hancock Shaker Village, MA.

Typeset by Bookworks Plus
Color separation by Excel Graphic Arts Ltd.
Printed and bound in Italy by Eurograph spa

8 7 6 5 4 3 2 1

Dedication

▲ ▲ ▲

To Meagan and Drew, my inspiration for books and life.

And to Colin Richmond, whose knowledge and reverence of the Shaker society
opened new avenues of appreciation beyond the academic.

© Jeff Greenberg/Hancock Shaker Village, MA

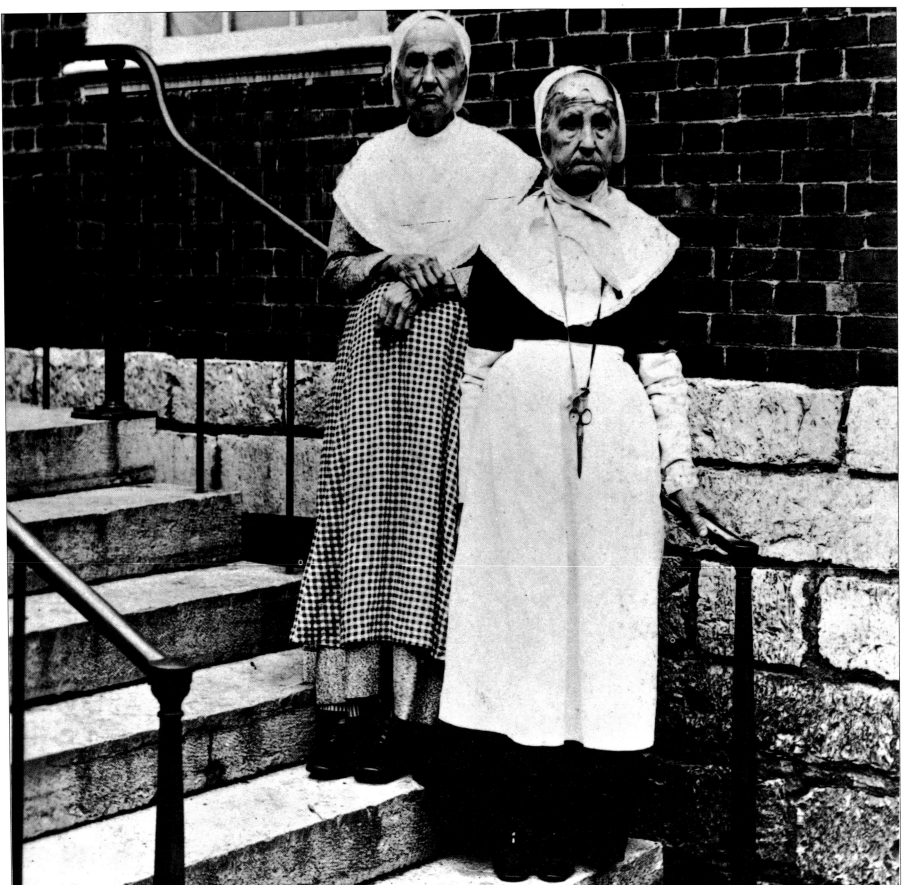

Courtesy The Winterthur Library, The Edward Deming Andrews Memorial Shaker Collection (both photos)

Introduction

▲▲▲

UNLIKELY ORIGINS

© George Goodwin

■ ABOVE: THIS FAN WAS PRESENTED TO ELIZA A. TAYLOR, THE DAUGHTER OF ANN LEE. OPPOSITE PAGE: SEPARATION OF THE SEXES IN THE SHAKER COMMUNITY RESULTED IN AESTHETICALLY PLEASING SYMMETRY IN ARCHITECTURE: TWO DOORS, ONE FOR MEN AND ANOTHER FOR WOMEN, AND EVEN TWIN STAIRCASES—BRETHREN AND SISTERS TRAVELING THE SAME DIRECTION BUT ALONG SEPARATE PATHS.

MENTION THE WORD "SHAKER" TODAY, AND THERE IS AN IMMEDIATE ASSOCIATION WITH QUALITY. The pristine lines of Shaker furniture, the impeccable symmetry of Shaker architecture, the unsurpassed craftsmanship of Shaker baskets or boxes all point to the same thing: a meticulous attention to quality. Such is the legacy of the Shaker society, a utopian communal order brought to America in the late eighteenth century and which, with only a handful of practicing members across the country, continues even now.

Shakers, officially known as the United Society of Believers in the First and Second Appearance of Christ, did not always have such an unblemished reputation. Nor did the Shaker millennial society, whose purpose was to pull away from the world, especially from its carnal urges, have origins that presaged success. In the unlikely personage of Ann Lee, the impoverished, illiterate daughter of a Manchester, England, blacksmith, Shakerism got its start.

Ann Lee's religious affiliation in England was with a sect of dissenters from the Anglican Church. More than a rote recital of ritual, this group's worship experience involved what its members believed to be a Pentecostal movement of the Holy Spirit—one demanding response. That response was a demonstrative emotional outpouring: paroxysms and trembles that soon had the practitioners labeled as "Shaking Quakers." The group's founders were James and Jane Wardley, former Quakers whose views were modified by radical French Calvinists called Camisards. Because of her religious convictions and the force of her personality, Ann Lee became the Wardleys' protégée. Soon, the couple was convinced that Ann, in fact, was none other than the second Messiah, and they turned all leadership over to her.

In fulfilling her leadership role to the Shaking Quakers, Ann was arrested around 1770 for disturbing the Sabbath. She was jailed, and from the inauspicious setting of her prison cell the concept of the Shaker society as we know it today was formulated. Here, Ann had a vision that lust was the world's fundamental evil. All of life's problems, she was shown, emanated from individuals' rapacious sexual appetites. In order to improve the human experience on earth, to eradicate man's problems, and strive for godlike perfection, persons must first abstain from sex. Only through a firm commitment to celibacy could anyone aspire to enter the kingdom of heaven. Or so went the vision.

For Ann, this vision was not the hardship it would have been for another. It required no radical change of heart. She already possessed a strong distaste for sex. Probably at her father's insistence and for economic reasons (she had to leave her Toad Lane home in Manchester at an early age to work in the cotton factories), Ann had to marry a local blacksmith, Abraham Stanley. She proceeded to give birth to four children, all of whom died either in infancy or early childhood. Ann never forgave herself for those deaths. She blamed the act

© Balthazar Korab

of procreation itself, viewing her submission to intercourse as the cause of her children's deaths. Her later vision of celibacy as the key to the kingdom of heaven, then, required no sacrifice; to Ann, it was a blessing.

Specifically, Ann's jail-cell vision entailed setting up a communal order of mutually-consenting celibates who would live in total innocence, men and women together as brother and sister, untouched by lust and its residual or related sins of violence and materialism. The logic held that, in forswearing a human impulse as basic and intense as the desire for sex, forswearing other impulses would follow in relatively easy fashion. Logistics—precisely where this celibate separatist society was to be established—were reserved for another vision, this one also from within a jail cell. In this second vision, Ann was convinced that America had been chosen by God as the homeland of a new society of celibates she was to head, the society known and respected today as Shaker.

If certain biblical precedents come to mind when considering Ann's experiences, those perhaps can be explained by, or at least help to explain, another of her convictions. The Wardleys weren't the only ones who believed Ann was the second Messiah. Ann did. She was convinced that she, along with Christ, was God's chosen spiritual head of a new and more perfect order on earth; that she was the mother incarnate of God's word. And with Jesus physically removed from earth, Ann believed it was up to her to establish this new order. When it's remembered that Ann's self-image depicted her as the female component of the godhead, it becomes less difficult to understand her Moseslike vision of leading her

■ THE ECONOMIC BASE OF SHAKER COMMUNITIES WAS AGRARIAN, MAKING BARNS SUCH AS THIS ONE AT WATERVLIET, NEW YORK, C. 1916, AMONG THE MOST IMPORTANT STRUCTURES IN A VILLAGE.

© George Goodwin/Watervliet, NY

© George Goodwin

people to a new land, or her parallel to the Apostle Paul in having spiritual adventures in jail, or even her Christlike breaking of the Sabbath and subsequent persecution. Believing herself to be not the same as Jesus, but his equal, Ann demonstrated an ego that surely could accommodate her placement on an equal footing with these earlier biblical giants. Ann saw herself as Jesus' completion—the final link necessary to establishing God's kingdom.

In 1774, at the age of thirty-eight, Ann Lee set out to implement her vision. She left England for America, traveling with eight followers, including her husband Abraham Stanley. At Ann's direction, the group dispersed in New York to seek work, survival taking priority, at least temporarily, over spirituality. Ann found a domestic job as a washerwoman, and in 1776, the Shakers convened once more to buy a small tract of land near Albany, at Wa-

■ THE SENSE OF BALANCE AND RIGHT PROPORTIONS THAT CHARACTERIZES SHAKER ARCHITECTURE MANIFESTS ITSELF IN VIRTUALLY ALL SHAKER HANDIWORK—EVEN GRAPHIC ILLUSTRATION USED AS MARKETING TOOLS FOR SHAKER PRODUCE, FRUITS, AND MEDICINE.

■ HANCOCK SHAKER VILLAGE'S MEETING HOUSE, C. 1793, ILLUSTRATES THE SHAKER AFFINITY IN ARCHITECTURE FOR ENGLISH ROOFS AND DORMER WINDOWS. ACCORDING TO THE SHAKER'S EARLY MILLENNIAL LAWS, AS PLACES OF WORSHIP, THE MEETINGHOUSES WERE TO BE THE ONLY BUILDINGS IN A VILLAGE TO DON WHITE PAINT—A RULE THAT LATER WAS RELAXED.

© Jeff Greenberg/Hancock Shaker Village, MA

tervliet. The first communal home was built at this site, but the building promptly was destroyed by fire. After five years in America, Mother Ann, as she now was called by her followers, had accrued no American converts. Furthermore, Stanley, unable to accept his wife's unswerving commitment to celibacy, left Ann to start a new life for himself. The tiny movement, its momentum thwarted at every turn, appeared destined to fail.

But soon the circumstances changed. The most felicitous event for the Shakers occurred in 1780, when Baptist minister Joseph Meacham encountered the group. Meacham was particularly impressed with Mother Ann's answer to allegations of being an equal to Jesus, and he was converted, bringing with him to the Shaker sect many members of his congregation. Flush with success, Ann took to traveling and preaching. Simultaneous with the increased attention she received was increased persecution. She was imprisoned for six months in 1780, the main charge being blasphemy. Ann spent the next two years preaching throughout New England, at the end of which time she was brutally assaulted. She returned to Watervliet where, in 1784, at the age of only forty-eight, she died.

After Mother Ann's death, the Believers turned to James Whittaker for leadership. Father James, as he respectfully was called, was only thirty-three years old at the time, but he had been with the group since its inception in Manchester. In fact, when James was just a boy he had kept Ann alive by feeding her wine and milk through a keyhole, while she was imprisoned. As Ann's successor, one of Father James's first priorities was to travel to other areas of the Northeast where clusters of Shakers were living, in search of new leaders.

At New Lebanon, New York, he found what he was looking for in Elder Joseph Meacham. Mother Ann herself had called Meacham "my first-born son in America." Under Father Meacham's leadership, New Lebanon became the hub of Shaker activity.

New Lebanon also was the first community of Believers to organize for communal living, finally bringing Mother Ann's dream to fruition, even though she was not alive to witness it. A meetinghouse for worship services was built there in 1785, and in 1787 members moved into their living quarters, sharing Christmas dinner as their first communal meal. The next Society order to organize was at Hancock, Massachusetts, in 1790. By 1794, eleven different orders were scattered across New England, but New Lebanon continued to function as the Shakers' central order and a model for all other communities. Working alongside Father Meacham as its spiritual leader was Lucy Wright—a testament to the fact that the Shakers went beyond just lip service and acted on the issue of equality between genders.

To this point, the basic principles of the Shakers had been confession of sins, celibacy, separation from the rest of the world, and communal ownership of property. Under Mea-

Courtesy The Winterthur Library: The Edward Deming Andrews Memorial Shaker Collection

■ SHAKER ART, LIMITED IN QUANTITY, IS COVETED BY TODAY'S COLLECTORS. THE ABOVE DRAWING WAS CREATED BY FATHER JAMES OF NEW LEBANON, NEW YORK, IN 1851 FOR JANE BLANCHARD AS A "TYPE OF MOTHER HANNAH'S POCKET HANDKERCHIEF."

© George Goodwin

■ AFTER MOTHER ANN'S DEATH, FATHER JAMES MEACHAM OF THE NEW LEBANON COMMUNITY CHANGED THE FRENETIC LEAPING DANCE THAT CHARACTERIZED THE SHAKERS AND GAVE THEM THEIR NAME, TO ONE MORE ORDERLY AND SUBDUED: A SIMPLE STEP FORWARD, STEP BACKWARD, DONE IN UNISON BY ALL BELIEVERS.

cham and Wright's leadership, though, the orders became more structured. Believers were now required to sign a formal covenant declaring allegiance. A governing system was instituted, too, with elders (of both sexes) holding most of the responsibility for the smooth operation of the community, and deacons and trustees (of both sexes as well) assisting.

The frenetic, leaping dance that prompted the "Shaking Quaker" sobriquet was abrogated. Meacham replaced it with a dance more in keeping with the overall demeanor of the Shakers: a simple step forward, step backward, dance that could be done in unison by all Believers. The orderliness and serenity which were to characterize the Shakers for posterity already was being fashioned.

After Meacham's death in 1796, Lucy Wright headed the New Lebanon community. She encouraged western expansion. In 1805, the ministry sent three missionaries into Kentucky and Ohio. Over the next two decades nine new Shaker communities were formed in the west: five in Ohio, two in Kentucky, one in western New York, and one in Indiana.

By 1840 the movement had reached its zenith. Shaker communities boasted a total population of about 6,000. But the momentum did not last. As early as 1875, settlements began to disband. Today only two working communities remain: those at Sabbathday Lake, Maine, and at Canterbury, New Hampshire.

The Shakers' decline in number belies their impact on our lives, particularly our work ethic. Their search for perfection was directed at their work, as well as their hearts. The beauty, detailing, and unpretentious grace and charm of Shaker products and structures are a legacy that can only leave the rest of the world inspired and challenged.

■ ALTHOUGH THE SHAKER LEGACY LIVES ON, PHOTOGRAPHS SUCH AS THIS DEPICTING THE LAST OF THE SHAKERS AT THE NOW-DISBANDED COMMUNITY OF HARVARD, MASSACHUSETTS, POIGNANTLY POINT TO LOSS, AS MEMBERSHIP DWINDLED AND COMMUNITIES WERE FORCED TO DISSOLVE.

Courtesy The Winterthur Library: The Edward Deming Andrews Memorial Shaker Collection

Last of the Shakers Harvard, Mass.

© Susanna Pashko/Envision/Hancock Shaker Village, MA

Chapter One

▲▲▲

ARCHITECTURE

"Do all your work as though you had a
thousand years to live, and as you would if
you knew you must die tomorrow."

MOTHER ANN LEE

© Mary Nemeth/Pleasant Hill, KY

■ ABOVE: THOUGH NOT THE HANDIWORK OF THE PREMIER SHAKER BUILDER, MOSES JOHNSON, THE BUILDINGS AT THE SHAKER VILLAGE OF PLEASANT HILL, KENTUCKY, NONETHELESS EXPRESS A SIMPLE, SYMMETRICAL DESIGN COMBINED WITH GEORGIAN ARCHITECTURAL ROOTS. OPPOSITE PAGE: SPIRALING UPWARDS AS IF TO HEAVEN, THE STAIRCASE IN THIS PLEASANT HILL BUILDING POSSESSES A SCULPTURAL GRACE THAT TRANSCENDS ITS UTILITY.

EVEN THE MOST VIRULENT DETRACTORS WOULD HAVE A HARD TIME ARGUING THE POINT TODAY: THE Shakers were ahead of their time. Long before "form follows function" became the credo of modern architecture, the Shakers were designing buildings on precisely that precept.

For this separatist religious sect, brought to America in 1774 by Mother Ann Lee, it was never a question of how a building should look, but how it must function. The idea of ornamentation for its own sake was abhorrent to the Shaker philosophy. Every aspect of a Shaker community, not just its architecture, expressed the idea of simplicity and modesty. No one person was to call attention to himself or herself, which meant that craftspersons, builders, and cabinetmakers were largely anonymous.

In regard to Shaker architecture, the logic behind this self-effacement was clear: Buildings could not be objects of beauty in their own right because that would be diverting worship away from God, to whom it rightfully belonged.

The only acceptable approach to architecture was from the position of need. In striving to design and build such adroitly functional structures, the Shakers refused to bow to the god of beauty. This mentality was mandated by Shaker Millennial Laws, which strictly prohibited "beadings, mouldings and cornices which are merely for fancy."

Amid such barebones simplicity, resplendent beauty still emerged. As proof, one need look no further than the twin spiral staircases, one for the Shaker brethren and the other for the sisters, in the Trustee's Office at the Shaker community at Pleasant Hill, Kentucky. Undulating with lulling rhythm and quiet dignity through the otherwise plain building, the staircases serve as a pièce de résistance. They also point to another of the Shakers' building directives: In all that you build, seek perfection.

The Shakers' quest for perfection was by an intense personal spiritual calling to reach deep within, in search of God and a measure of work worthy of Him. Ironically, in pursuing perfection the Shakers cancelled out their own attempts to ignore aesthetics.

No wonder Shaker architecture is beautiful. In its simplicity, orderliness, and craftsmanship, it may represent man's best shot at perfection. Granted, for the Shakers it was the work ethic and not the aesthetic that counted. And granted, the sense of serenity and rightness that pervades their architecture was only a residual effect of following Mother Ann's admonition to "put your hands to work and hearts to God." But byproduct or not, an almost prescient "less is more" beauty exists in Shaker architecture that cannot be denied. Vestiges of the Believers' building efforts are prized today not only for their inherent qualities of good design and construction, but as tangible proof of people's best—a reminder of what it means to pursue a task with a total commitment to excellence.

© William Roger Morgan/Envision/Pleasant Hill, KY

■ ABOVE: BUILT BY MOSES JOHNSON IN 1794 AND STILL AMAZINGLY UNCHANGED, THE MEETING HOUSE AT SABBATHDAY LAKE, MAINE, IS THE BEST EXTANT EXAMPLE OF JOHNSON'S ARCHITECTURE. IT CONTINUES TO BE USED EVEN TODAY FOR WORSHIP SERVICES BY THE REMAINING SMALL GROUP OF BELIEVERS. OPPOSITE PAGE, ABOVE: A FIRE DESTROYED THE C. 1786 MEETINGHOUSE BUILT BY JOHNSON AT NEW LEBANON, NEW YORK. OPPOSITE PAGE, BELOW: IN 1824 A NEARLY IDENTICAL SECOND STRUCTURE WAS ERECTED.

© Brian Vanden Brink/Sabbathday Lake, ME

▲ THE MEETINGHOUSE

The Believers' insistence on considering function first in their architecture determined what kinds of structures would be represented in a Shaker community. Obviously there had to be a place to congregate for worship. Meetinghouses served this purpose and were the first, and most highly esteemed, buildings constructed in a settlement. Because of the sacrosanct nature of the meetinghouse, white paint was reserved exclusively for it, at least in the early communities. Later, as orders became more lax, other buildings also were painted white, including the Spinning House and Boys' Shop at Sabbathday Lake, for example. The original Millennial Laws, however, made it clear that white, a symbol of purity, was to be used only on churches.

▲ MOSES JOHNSON

As the most influential settlement, New Lebanon, New York, served as an architectural prototype for other colonies. Master builder Moses Johnson built the meetinghouse there, as well as nine more in other Shaker villages. He is considered the premier Shaker builder.

Moses Johnson was born in 1752, but his place of birth is unknown. He was living in the vicinity of Enfield, New Hampshire, in 1782 when Shaker activity began there. In October of that year, Johnson joined the group of Believers with his wife and three children and was one of the original signers of the Enfield Covenant. His credentials as an expert carpenter and joiner were already established because, at the age of thirty-three, he was selected by the Shaker elders to travel to New Lebanon, more than two hundred miles (320 km) away, to frame that community's meetinghouse.

He supervised the construction of the building, which was completed by January 29, 1786, when the first service was held in it. (The extant New Lebanon meetinghouse that tourists see today is not Johnson's original, but was built in the style of the original in 1824, nearly forty years after the first.)

From there, Johnson followed a hectic agenda of travel to other Shaker communities in need of construction. He did not necessarily remain in each one for the duration of the building project, but long enough to provide the specifications and initiate the construction process under his supervision. All materials used in Johnson's meetinghouses were made or obtained from nature by the Shakers (Shaker-forged nails and Shaker-cut logs, for example), and Shaker brethren provided the labor for the construction itself. Leaving the building details in capable hands, Johnson was able to travel to the next area needing a meetinghouse. In 1791, Johnson went to Watervliet (the original Shaker settlement in the United States) and began work on the church there in March. Assisted in the construction by three brethren,

Brothers Moses Mixer, Stephen Markham, and John Bruce, he was able to leave Watervliet in June to begin the meetinghouse at Enfield, Connecticut.

The ten Shaker meetinghouses attributed to Johnson are, chronologically according to construction dates: New Lebanon, New York; Hancock, Massachusetts; Watervliet, New York; Enfield, Connecticut, Harvard, Massachusetts; Canterbury, New Hampshire; Shirley, Massachusetts; Enfield, New Hampshire; Alfred, Maine; and Sabbathday Lake, Maine. Johnson is documented as the builder of seven of the meetinghouses. Those at Hancock, Alfred, and Sabbathday Lake are attributed to him as a result of the Shaker oral tradition. The inability to make conclusive attribution stems from the Shakers' downplay of the individual; the work, not the worker, was what deserved merit and remembrance. The only reason for documenting a building's designer was for efficiency in business records, not for personal praise or posterity.

© George Goodwin/Mount Lebanon, NY

© George Goodwin/Mount Lebanon, NY

© Kenneth Martin/Amstock/Hancock Shaker Village, MA

■ WITH ITS CRISPLY DEFINED ENGLISH-STYLE GAMBREL ROOF AND WHITE CLAPBOARD FACADE, THE C.1793 MEETINGHOUSE AT HANCOCK SHAKER VILLAGE CUTS A STRIKING SILHOUETTE AGAINST THE OPEN SKY.

Johnson designed all of his churches as simple clapboard rectangles. In addition to the white paint, which distinguished them from other structures in a Shaker community, Johnson's meetinghouses were further set apart by the unique silhouette of a gambrel roof. In crowning his churches with this type of hipped roof instead of the expected gable found elsewhere in a community, Johnson stirred later speculation that his architecture showed a Dutch Colonial influence. Gambrel roofs, indeed, are a key architectural trait of Dutch buildings in the Hudson River Valley, but the British also employed this building form. However, Johnson's interpretation of a gambrel roof, with its equal-sized pitches, more nearly approximates the English version, which had a long lower pitch and short top one, with deep eaves.

The front of each of Johnson's meetinghouses had separate entrances for brethren and sisters. The narrow ends each had a single door—one for the female ministry, the other for the male. This need for separate but equal facilities is directly accountable for the symmetry that characterizes Shaker architecture; it is a sterling example of form following function.

The placement of windows was balanced, too, a result of the need for separate entries: two windows on either side of the doors, another three in between them. The first or lower pitch of Johnson's roofs was punctuated by three dormer windows, on both the front and back of the buildings. Another characteristic feature of his architecture was a pair of flanking chimneys at either end of the meetinghouse. Chimneys typically accommodated, not fireplaces, but small woodburning stoves built by the Shakers.

Just as function determined the appearance of the building's facade, so did it dictate how the structure was integrated into the landscape. A white picket fence surrounded the meetinghouse, separating it from other structures, and at either end of the fence were two gates—one for the sisters, one for the brethren. The gates were set exactly opposite the two entry doors, further enhancing the balance and its attendant sense of serenity.

Inside, the meetinghouse featured a large assembly hall. Millennial Laws dictated that the interior woodwork be painted a "bluish shade," meaning a dark blue-green. The original paint can still be seen in the meetinghouse at Sabbathday Lake—the best intact example of Johnson's architecture, still unchanged since he built the structure in 1794, and still used as a Shaker church today. Blue trim paint also has been retained at the Canterbury, New Hampshire, meetinghouse, another surviving piece of Johnson's architecture. The blue featured in Canterbury's assembly room is lighter than the original color, however—the result of a paint job executed in 1875 by a resident elder. The blue trim found upstairs at Canterbury is darker and is Johnson's original, as are the unusual interior window shutters, which ingeniously close by sliding into the walls.

The interiors of all of Johnson's meetinghouses were studies in contrast. The dark blue paint on woodwork served as a sharp counterpoint to the walls, which were inevitably covered in pristine white plaster. Both the stark white and deep blue were underscored by the yellowish hue of the wood floors.

Where color left off, visual interest was picked up by the architectural elements. Wooden beams secured at the wall by boxed knee braces spanned the ceiling, and wainscoting topped with a chair rail covered the lower walls up to the window sills.

Shakers were zealots about order—everything had a place, including the furniture, and nothing was to be left out of place for long. At the end of worship, when chairs no longer were being used for sitting, Believers would pick them up and hang them on the wall—upside down, to prevent dust from settling on the seat. Thus, a strip of pegboard with wooden pegs for hanging items became a key architectural feature, not only of the meetinghouse, but of every Shaker building. In the assembly hall, the pegboards were located on the walls about five feet (1.5 m) off the floor.

© Balthazar Korab

■ ARCHWAYS WERE A DISTINGUISHING BUILDING TRAIT OF KENTUCKY'S SHAKER ARCHITECTURE, CLEARLY SEPARATING THAT REGION'S DESIGN FROM THE MORE RECTILINEAR MODES OF NEW ENGLAND AND NEW YORK.

■ *BELOW:* THE STRONG HORIZONTAL SWEEP OF EXPOSED CEILING BEAMS IN THE SABBATHDAY LAKE MEETINGHOUSE IS REPEATED BELOW IN THE ELONGATED BENCH SEATING. *OPPOSITE PAGE, ABOVE:* AT THE SOUTH UNION, KENTUCKY, FAMILY DWELLING, THE ARCH-SHAPED WOOD TRIM AROUND THE DOORS IS A TELLING SIGN OF THE REGIONAL ARCHITECTURAL PREFERENCE FOR ARCHES. SEPARATE STAIRWAYS FOR SISTERS AND BRETHREN CREATE A FORMAL BALANCE. *OPPOSITE PAGE, BELOW:* THE ARCHES SOFTEN THE OTHERWISE POTENTIALLY HARD-EDGED FEEL OF THE SPACE.

The only fixed furniture in the assembly room were two or three raised levels of benches. Painted rich brown, these graced the front of the room and were reserved for visitors. Otherwise, the room was unencumbered. No vertical support posts marred the openness, thanks to huge trusses supporting the roof.

In addition to the meetinghouses at Sabbathday Lake, Maine, and Canterbury, New Hampshire, only one of Moses Johnson's original structures still stands. It is the meetinghouse from Shirley, Massachusetts, which was moved in 1962 to the Hancock Shaker Village, where it stands on the site originally occupied by that village's church. Beautifully restored, it is the only surviving example of Johnson's architecture to retain its original interior staircase.

© Brian Vanden Brink/Sabbathday Lake, ME

© Richard Day/Shakertown at South Union, KY

▲ KENTUCKY ARCHITECTURE
Moses Johnson never made it outside of New England to lend a hand in the design of the Shaker communities to the West. Consequently, the architecture in Kentucky, which had a larger Shaker population than any other state outside of New York, is different.

For one thing, the warmer climate necessitated some differences in how buildings were designed. For optimum coolness during the warm months, buildings in Kentucky's Shaker villages were given taller ceilings and breezier hallways than their low-slung, compact counterparts to the East.

Another distinguishing feature of the Kentucky architecture has nothing to do with function but is, instead, a purely subjective visual preference. Kentucky Shakers liked arches. Whenever possible, they incorporated this building motif into their designs for an overall softer, less hard-edged look. Doorways, for example, weren't rectilinear but were arched. At the Center Family Dwelling at South Union, Kentucky, woodwork takes the shape of a large half-moon—the classic arch, dominating the upper portion of a hallway wall opening onto a meeting room.

© Balthazar Korab

© William Roger Morgan/Envision/Pleasant Hill, KY

■ *PREVIOUS PAGE: AS THE HUB OF THE SHAKER WORLD, THE NEW LEBANON, NEW YORK, COMMUNITY SET RELIGIOUS POLICY FOR ALL BELIEVERS. THE MOST IMPORTANT BUILDINGS IN THE VILLAGE WERE THE MEETINGHOUSES, SHOWN HERE. ABOVE: BRETHREN AND SISTERS LIVED UNDER A SINGLE ROOF IN DWELLING HOUSES SUCH AS THIS C.1834 LIMESTONE ONE AT PLEASANT HILL, WHICH IS CONSIDERED AMONG THE BEST ARCHITECTURAL TYPE OF THE GENRE. INTERACTION BETWEEN GENDERS WAS MINIMAL, HOWEVER, DUE TO SEGREGATED LIVING ARRANGEMENTS AT OPPOSITE ENDS OF THE BUILDING, WHICH INCLUDED SEPARATE OUTSIDE ENTRANCES.*

▲ DWELLING

One of the most remarkable aspects of the Shakers was not their doctrine of celibacy, but the practice of this doctrine by Believers of both sexes within close proximity of the opposite sex. One elder compared the Shaker arrangement of sisters and brethren to "monks and nuns, without the bolts and bars."

Shaker men and women were not segregated according to gender in their living arrangements. Both sexes lived together under one roof. In fact, the Shakers were so confident of their convictions of celibacy and their resistance to temptation that they not only lived together in a single dwelling, but both sexes occupied a single floor within a dwelling. Although a communal house may have spanned several stories, instead of relegating men to one floor and women to another, the Shakers separated the sexes only by wings, with brethren rooming at one end of the building and sisters at the other.

Except for the ministry, the male and female elders who provided primary leadership for the community, all Believers lived communally in dwellings. The ministry lived apart in ministry shops. This arrangement was not so much a privilege of power as it was an assurance that the spiritual leaders would retain their objectivity in settling disputes, making decisions, and counseling other Believers.

The buildings shared by the main body of Believers were referred to as dwellings, not homes, and they were paragons of simplicity. As with meetinghouses and, really, all Shaker structures, these communal homes were designed for high-efficiency performance. No frills, no extra comforts or embellishments. As with the meetinghouses, the dwellings' architecture illustrated an abiding concern for getting it right—perfecting the line, integrating multifunctional built-ins into the interiors as inconspicuously as possible.

The dwellings showed the influence of Georgian architecture, that being the style the original Shakers from England knew best. Interpreted by the Shakers, Georgian design became even more austere and pared down, especially the interiors.

Dwellings were simple rectangles, symmetrical because of the need for two of everything, including two separate entry doors and two separate staircases. These communal homes spanned several stories, had dormer windows and transoms, and were planned so that brethren could occupy rooms on one side of each floor, with sisters on the other. Dormitory style, several persons occupied each "retiring room" or bedroom.

Building materials varied according to the region of the community or "family," as these settlements were called. Red-painted woods or brick were favored at Watervliet, whereas white-painted woods or stone were the materials of choice at New Lebanon. Shaker law even dictated the paint colors. Wooden buildings on the street were to be lightest in color,

Courtesy The Henry Francis du Pont Winterthur Museum

while those farther back were to be red, gray, or brown. By the end of the nineteenth century, however, this rule was no longer observed.

Three of the most sophisticated dwellings were at Enfield, New Hampshire; Pleasant Hill, Kentucky; and South Union, Kentucky. The Enfield dwelling towered four full stories and two half stories high. Measuring one hundred feet (30 m) long by fifty-six feet (17 m) wide, it was built of finished granite blocks. These were not only cemented together but, for further durability, were secured with iron trunnels. In its outstanding construction and accompanying beauty, the Enfield dwelling was considered one of the state's preeminent examples of fine architecture.

■ RETIRING ROOMS, AS THE SHAKER DORM-STYLE BEDROOMS WERE KNOWN, WERE STUDIES IN EFFICIENCY, FURNISHED ONLY WITH ESSENTIAL FREE-STANDING PIECES, SINCE THE BUILT-IN STORAGE CABINETS SUFFICED FOR MOST NEEDS.

© Richard Day/Shakertown at South Union, KY

■ AT SOUTH UNION, KENTUCKY, THE CENTER FAMILY DWELLING DEVIATED A BIT FROM THE SHAKER NORM OF A FACADE WITH TWO SEPARATE ENTRANCES. HERE, TWO SEPARATE SETS OF STEPS LEADING TO THE MAIN DOOR SERVED THE SAME PURPOSE. BUILT ENTIRELY OF RED BRICK, THE BUILDING WAS COMPLETED IN 1824.

At Pleasant Hill, the limestone dwelling took ten years to build, finally reaching completion in 1834. It includes more than forty rooms on four stories, with the kitchen, food cellars, and ministry's private dining area in the basement. The first floor housed the communal dining hall, and the central kitchen and baking rooms. On each of the first and second floors were six retiring rooms and two dressing rooms. Additionally, the second floor included a large meeting room and several small rooms, which comprised an infirmary. Interestingly, the building has a small cupola protruding off-center at the roofline. The cupola opens onto what amounts to a balustraded widow's walk, another unusual feature for a Shaker building.

The South Union dwelling, whose date stone above the second story's center window indicates completion in 1824, was built entirely of red brick. Unlike most dwellings, it did not allow for separate doorways for the sexes, but had a single front entrance with two sets of stairs. A white picket fence, a feature of nearly all dwellings, handsomely surrounded it. Both the South Union and Pleasant Hill dwellings had dark exterior shutters flanking their multilighted, small-paned windows, which could fold inward to protect the glass when necessary. Both Kentucky dwellings also featured windows that were capped with lintels, stones inset horizontally into the exterior walls.

The interiors of dwellings resembled the insides of meetinghouses, the only significant difference being an even greater number of built-ins and, of course, features unique to a home, such as a kitchen and dining room. Walls were of white plaster, and soft, warm wood such as butternut was used for wainscoting and trim. Millennial Laws required that "floors in dwellings, if stained at all, should be of reddish yellow." Pegboards for hanging cloaks, hats, bonnets, pipes, candlesticks, chairs, and baskets—whatever needed a home—were a mainstay, along with built-in cupboards and drawers made entirely of wood (even the drawer and cabinet pulls).

In the bedrooms or retiring rooms, however, each person did not have his or her own built-in dresser or storage shelves. Only one small cupboard was included in each room, for possessions were few and none were held personally, all being communally owned.

■ *ABOVE:* SHAKER BEDROOMS CONTAINED ONLY THE BARE ESSENTIALS: A BED, BUILT-IN CUPBOARDS, A CHAIR, A DRESSER, AND A STOVE FOR WARMTH. *LEFT:* SHAKER BEDS, SUCH AS THIS ONE FROM SOUTH UNION, WERE A DEPARTURE FROM THE MASSIVE, FOUR-POSTER, CANOPIED BEDS OF THE DAY.

© George Goodwin/Mount Lebanon, NY

■ *ABOVE:* EVEN A STRICTLY UTILITARIAN SHAKER FEATURE SUCH AS THIS DRYING RACK, EXPRESSED AN ARCHITECTURAL AESTHETIC OF SPARTAN PURITY AND RIVETING PRESENCE. *RIGHT:* BELIEVERS WERE ESSENTIALLY INDUSTRIOUS, DRAWING ON EACH CHORE—EVEN THE LABORIOUS TASK OF LAUNDERING, WHICH WAS PERFORMED IN SPECIFIC LAUNDRY ROOMS SUCH AS THIS ONE IN HANCOCK, MASSACHUSETTS— AS AN OPPORTUNITY TO DO THEIR BEST AS A MEANS OF SERVING GOD.

The idea behind a profuse number of built-ins throughout the public spaces of a dwelling was order and convenience, and also, saving space. Because the Shakers lived together as a group, easily accessible storage was imperative. Order—a place for everything—wasn't so much an ideal as it was a pragmatic solution: With many hands sharing in the work, it was essential that household items have permanent storage areas known by all.

The number of cabinets and drawers and their sizes depended on the room's function. In an eight-foot- (24-m-) high dining room, cabinets might extend the entire eight feet. When

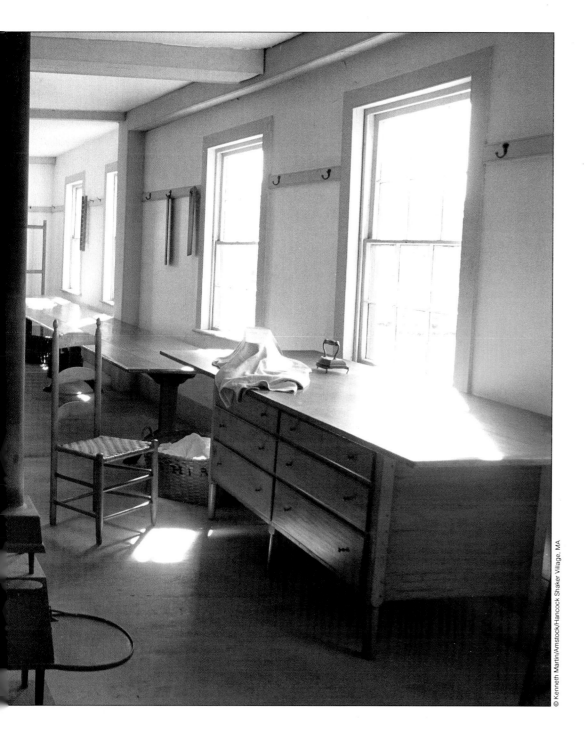

© Kenneth Martin/Amstock/Hancock Shaker Village, MA

it was necessary to build shelves higher than the average person's height, small steps were provided. Long before the invention of computers, then, the Shakers designed on the "user friendly" principle.

In addition to dictating the color of a dwelling's floors, Millennial Laws specified that "varnish, if used in dwelling houses, may be used only to the moveables therein . . . no ceilings or mouldings may be varnished." Varnish was permissible for use on banisters and handrails, though.

▲ BARNS

The Shaker society was agricultural. Believers were self-sufficient, raising their own crops and animals. On an almost equal footing with dwellings, then, were barns, for these structures were essential to the family's function. Barns were as neat and orderly, and very nearly as clean, as dwellings. No indulgence of slovenly habits was permitted, even in the stewardship of livestock. A visit today to one of the remaining old barns underscores the point: Whereas moldy, musty smells permeate most aging barns, the Shaker version smells decidedly fresh and clean. Traces of clover linger in the air.

Always practical, the Shakers situated their barns into a hillside whenever geography permitted. This enabled entry from different levels and simplified the haying process considerably, enabling bails to be pitched down into the barn instead of up.

One of the most outstanding Shaker barns is the Hancock, Massachusetts's Round Barn. It, too, features great ingenuity in its functional design. A perfect circle, the barn consists of a central two-story section made of stone. A twelve-sided wooden level caps the stone, and above it rises a hexagonal bell tower. The round shape, so aesthetically pleasing and distinctive by today's standards, originated out of need. The Shakers wanted to be able to drive a haytruck inside of the barn for unloading, then out again through the same door. The circular shape facilitated that, with the hay unloaded in the center of the barn as the truck drove through.

Because of their importance to the community, the barns were extremely large. The New Lebanon barn was 296 feet (90 m) long, fifty feet (15 m) wide, and five stories high. Built into a hillside, it had upper levels for storage of grain and hay, with cows kept in stalls on the main level. A huge manure pit was at one end, filled by a system of buckets pulled around a half-circle catwalk on the main level where the animals were, and then emptied into the level below. In addition to the huge barns, the Shakers built auxiliary structures for the storage of wagons and carts.

▲ OTHER BUILDINGS

As Shaker industries flourished, special buildings were required to serve as shops. One of the most important of these was the blacksmith shop, for all the nails, iron railings, and rough-and-finish hardware used in construction were made here, in addition to the essential, more expected horseshoes and wagon wheels. Even in this most functional of shops exquisite craftsmanship and detailing were an integral part of the architecture. New Lebanon's blacksmith shop, built in 1846, echoes the careful workmanship of what was being produced in the shop: Quorin stones dress the corners of the facade, while lintels crown the windows and doors.

© Jeff Greenberg/Hancock Shaker Village, MA.

■ *OPPOSITE PAGE:* BUILT IN 1826, THE ROUND STONE BARN OF THE SHAKER VILLAGE OF HANCOCK, MASSACHUSETTS, IS ONE OF THE MOST RENOWNED EXAMPLES OF SHAKER ARCHITECTURE. INORDINATELY CLEAN AND SWEET-SMELLING IN COMPARISON TO BARNS OF "THE WORLD," THIS SHAKER FACILITY FEATURED A DRAMATIC ROUND SHAPE AS A PRACTICAL SOLUTION TO A PROBLEM: TRUCKS COULD DRIVE IN AND DROP OFF HAY IN THE CENTER, THEN EXIT THROUGH THE SAME DOOR FROM WHICH THEY ENTERED. *ABOVE:* THE HANCOCK BARN FEATURED A CENTRAL, TWO-STORY STONE SECTION CAPPED BY A TWELVE-SIDED WOODEN TIER, WHICH, IN TURN, WAS SURMOUNTED BY A HEXAGONAL BELL TOWER.

© Jeff Greenberg/Hancock Shaker Village, MA

■ SHAKER COMMUNITIES WERE CIRCUMSCRIBED BY PICTURESQUE WHITE PICKET FENCES. SHOWN IN THE BACKGROUND ARE THE LAUNDRY AND MACHINE SHOP AT HANCOCK, MASSACHUSETTS.

The best approach to determining the kinds of buildings that were present in a Shaker community is simply to look at a few typical orders. The village at Hancock, Massachusetts, included a meetinghouse, dwellings, a garden-tool shed, laundry and machine shops, a poultry house, a dairy, a tanning house, and the famous round stone barn. The Canterbury, New Hampshire, village included a girls' house and boys' house; a schoolhouse; a meetinghouse; ministry shops; a business office; and dairy barns and workshops, including garden-seed rooms, a bake shop, a weaving room, a spin shop, a print shop, a blacksmith's shop, a butcher shop, a shoemaker's shop, a joiner's shop, a cider mill, and still others. The Shakers were fond of maple trees, and in the New England settlements their villages were given order and splendor with neat rows of the deciduous trees, that softened and colored the townscape.

▲ **CONVENIENCES** Confusing the Shakers with the Amish, popular mythology often depicts the Society of Believers as shunning technology or anything that smacks of modernity. Nothing could be farther from the truth. The Shakers heartily embraced new inventions, seeing them as avenues to greater productivity and a more streamlined way of life. No ox-drawn plows furrowed Shaker fields once the tractor was invented, enabling the job to be done in half the time.

This penchant for efficiency and openness to new and better ways manifested itself in Shaker architecture. Shaker buildings demonstrate an amazingly advanced degree of inventiveness, with a plethora of step-saving designs and cleverly engineered conveniences.

© Kenneth Martin/Amstock/Hancock Shaker Village, MA

■ SHAKERS HAD LITTLE PATIENCE FOR SPENDING UNNECESSARY TIME AND ENERGY ON CHORES, WHEN THEY COULD BE SPENDING IT WORSHIPPING GOD. CONSEQUENTLY, THEY USED THEIR INGENUITY AS A WAY TO SPEED UP THE EVERYDAY CHORES OF LIFE. ONE EXAMPLE OF THIS IS SEEN IN THE DUMB WAITER IN THE HANCOCK DINING ROOM.

For the Church Family Dwelling at Hancock, Massachusetts, Elder William Deming (1779–1849) designed the dining room to include a pair of dumbwaiters. Sparing the sisters considerable time and steps in serving meals, the dumbwaiters meant that "the victuals is conveyed up [from the basement kitchen] into the dining rooms by means of two sliding cupboards," wrote Elder Deming.

Opposed though they were to contrived ornamentation or anything deliberately constructed for appearances only, the Shakers were great proponents of natural beauty. They were lovers of trees, light, and air. As such, they were constantly inventing new ways to bring sunshine and fresh air into their buildings. In the Church Family Dwelling at Hancock, a window was cut into an interior wall to let sunlight drench a stairwell on the opposite side of the space. Even in their barns, the Shakers were known to add a clerestory so that its windows could bring in more natural light.

■ THRIVING ON NATURAL LIGHT, THE SHAKERS WENT TO GREAT LENGTHS TO ADD WINDOWS TO EVEN THE MOST UNLIKELY PLACES, A POINT PROVEN BY THE SUNSHINE FLOODING INTO THE INTERIOR OF THE ROUND STONE BARN AT HANCOCK.

© Kenneth Martin/Amstock/Hancock Shaker Village, MA

© Jeff Greenberg/Hancock Shaker Village. MA

■ ANOTHER WINDOW IN THE HANCOCK BARN ADMITS A VIEW OF THE PRISTINE STONE DWELLING HOUSE BEYOND.

Long before skylights became a hot building trend, the Shakers were incorporating them into their architecture. They situated skylights in their attics not only to bring in light, but to avoid danger: The natural light eliminated the need for candles and lanterns and the fire hazard these light sources posed. At the Hancock Shaker Village, double skylights were built into the two upper stories of the Church Family Dwelling. Both stories were used as attics, and in the upper attic, skylights were placed in the roof and floor. Light that was admitted through the rooftop skylight was able to filter through the skylight in the floor, illuminating the second attic below.

Courtesy The Henry Francis du Pont Winterthur Museum

■ ABOVE: A MAJOR ARCHITECTURAL FEATURE OF SHAKER INTERIORS ARE BUILT-IN CUPBOARDS. SPANNING FROM FLOOR TO CEILING, THEY ENSURED ORDER: A PLACE FOR EVERYTHING—A PRIORITY IN THE SHAKER RELIGION AS A MEANS OF MINIMIZING THE CLUTTER OF THE WORLD, WHICH DISTRACTED FROM WORSHIPPING GOD. OPPOSITE PAGE: IN ADDITION TO THE UBIQUITOUS BUILT-IN CUPBOARDS THAT LINED INTERIOR WALLS, ANOTHER IDENTIFYING TRAIT ENSURING THE DISPOSAL OF OBJECTS IN AN ORDERLY FASHION WERE WALL-MOUNTED PEGS.

The Shakers' love of light also is illustrated in the dining room of Hancock's Church Family Dwelling. The room contains ninety-five windows, each with twenty-four lights (panes of glass) to bring in sunlight from the east, west, and south. While there is nothing ingenious in that alone, a marked inventiveness can be found in the window construction. The windows were designed with removable sashes for easy washing and repair—an engineering feat that made especially good sense when considering the uppermost, hard-to-reach windows. The sash was held in position by a slender wood strip that was fastened onto the frame with wooden thumbscrews. To remove the sash for washing or maintenance, it was simply a matter of removing the thumbscrews and wood strips.

As much as the Shakers enjoyed natural light, so did they appreciate a good flow of fresh air. Buildings were designed with ventilation as a significant priority, not an afterthought or luxury. Baseboards were bored with holes to allow for the circulation of air at floor level. Overhead ventilation was provided through transoms, which were built above most doors. At the Canaan Upper Family Dwelling, transoms took the form of apertures with swinging panels above the doorway.

Nothing sums up the Shakers' bent on order and convenience better or more succinctly than the ubiquitous pegboards that circumscribed virtually every room. Pulling a close second place as exponents of order are built-in cupboards. The Shakers were not the first to construct with built-ins, but they were unmatched in terms of the quantity of built-ins used. The attic in a dwelling in Canterbury, New Hampshire, featured wall-to-wall built-in storage: six closets, fourteen cupboards, 101 drawers, and two storage areas under the eaves.

Pegboards and built-in cupboards and drawers weren't the only forms of storage used by the Shakers. Confronted with dead space or an unusual building circumstance, the Shakers literally invented a way around the problem, creating a one-of-a-kind design as need dictated. When the ministry shop at Sabbathday Lake, Maine, was remodeled with a pitched roof replacing the old flat one, the Shakers seized the opportunity to design a new storage unit geared to the triangular-shaped roofline. The resulting inverted V-shaped wooden unit allowed for maximum storage within limited space. Ahead of its time, Shaker architecture was multi-functional and eminently efficient, with no wasted space.

Whenever it could, Shaker architecture helped to ease the work load. For instance, raising the base of a staircase banister off the floor a few inches meant an easier time sweeping and mopping. Architecture also showed an economy of elements: Chimney flues joined together below the roofline to become one above the roof. And again ahead of its time, Shaker architecture called for water power to be harnessed, whenever possible.

© MacDonald Photography/Envision/Hancock Shaker Village, MA

Chapter Two

▲▲▲

FURNITURE

"Put your hands to work and your
hearts to God."

MOTHER ANN LEE

© Jeanetta Ho/Dunham Tavern Museum Collection

■ BY FAR THE MOST COMMON FURNISHING CRAFTED BY THE SHAKERS WAS THE LADDER-BACK CHAIR—A COMMODITY PRODUCED FOR TRADE WITH THE WORLD.

AFTER ONLY SEEING A FEW PIECES OF SHAKER FURNITURE, EVEN THOSE WITHOUT EXPERTISE IN antiques or cabinetmaking have no trouble singling out the Shaker style, if not the authentic article, from the herd.

Shaker furnishings were crafted from the philosophical perspective that "all things must be made . . . according to their order and use. All work done, or things made in the church, ought to be faithfully and well done, but plain and without superfluity—neither too high nor too low." Father Joseph Meacham, who replaced Mother Ann as the Shaker's spiritual leader and organized the Millennial Church, set the standard not only for furniture making, but for all Shaker enterprise in *Way-Marks* (1790).

From the beginning, utilitarianism was the first and most important hallmark of Shaker furnishings. Even so, it was a functionalism proving "that which has in itself the highest use possesses the greatest beauty."

A favorite Shaker saying was "order is heaven's first law"—and that the Shakers took this to heart is undoubtable, based on the purity of line in their furniture design.

Besides an inherent beauty resulting from this trenchant reduction to essences, to the core utility and order of a furnishing, Shaker furniture possesses other, less subjective traits of distinction.

Shaker furnishings combine seemingly incongruous characteristics. Communal living required portable furniture, so Shaker furnishings needed to be light in scale and weight. Chairs, in particular, had to be light enough to be hung, en masse, from pegboards. Consequently, furnishings possessed a delicate, almost reedy, appearance. At the same time, however, they were extremely well made, giving them an underlying sturdiness that is evident even at a glance.

Credit for this latter quality must be attributed to the Shakers' communal lifestyle. All craftsmanship including furniture making was a community enterprise executed in an almost assembly-line procedure in the workshops. No one was permitted a solo effort, regardless of talent.

A natural outgrowth of the team effort was uniformity, whether the product was a chair or a pincushion. Not only did Shaker furnishings share common features of design and construction but, more importantly, of excellence. The Shakers put to practice the words of one of their songs: "Labor is worship and prayer." Their religious drive for perfection was collectively harnessed by workers into producing consistently outstanding work.

The Shakers settled only for the best tools, and during the peak of their furniture industry—the first half of the nineteenth century—produced some of the most skillfully sawed, planed, turned, and pegged furniture ever made by any joiner. Inspired by notions such as purity and humility, the Shaker cabinetmakers unwittingly communicated a chaste, spiritual quality in what they produced.

Although furnishings were constructed uniformly, ensuring the egalitarian principle that no man or woman should have better than the rest, there was variety in size. The Shakers were too pragmatic and efficient to ignore the fact that different body types did not lend themselves to the same size furniture. As with their architecture, the Believers were ahead of their time with furnishings as well. They adapted shapes to fit the human form, anticipating the principles of ergonomic design long before that term became a furniture industry buzzword. Like architecture, Shaker furniture was crafted so that form followed function—or, put another way, form followed fit and fit dictated form.

Together, the two Shaker religious convictions—pursuing perfection and avoiding superfluous decoration—led to the creation of a homogenous blend of architecture and furniture. Here, too, the Believers were advanced for their age. Their convictions were like the approach of architect Frank Lloyd Wright, "to incorporate as organic architecture—so far as possible—furnishings, making them one with the building, and designing them in simple terms. Again straight lines and rectilinear forms."

It is not surprising that Shaker furniture is prized today by antiques collectors and aficionados of contemporary design. Those with a penchant for modernism appreciate economy of line—a design approach mastered by the Believers. In its near-Spartan simplicity, Shaker furniture is unmatched by virtually any other style.

© Philip M. Zito/Dunham Tavern Museum Collection

■ PIN CUSHIONS WERE A WELL-KNOWN SHAKER ITEM PRODUCED FOR THE OUTSIDE WORLD BY THE SHAKER SISTERS.

■ ALTHOUGH THE SHAKERS CANNOT TAKE CREDIT FOR INVENTING THE ROCKING CHAIR, THEY WERE AMONG THE FIRST IN AMERICA TO EQUIP CHAIRS WITH ROCKERS. THE FIRST ROCKING CHAIRS WERE BUILT FOR THE ILL OR ELDERLY, BUT AFTER THE TURN OF THE FIRST DECADE OF THE 1800S, THEY BECAME A STANDARD APPOINTMENT FOR BELIEVERS' RETIRING ROOMS.

© Philip M. Zito/Golden Lamb, OH

▲ **CHAIRS**   Shaker cabinetmakers were especially prolific at producing chairs, and for an obvious reason: More chairs were required within the community than any other type of furnishing. There was another reason, though. Chairmaking was not limited to internal demand. Beginning with the Shaker community at New Lebanon, the production of chairs became an industry selling to the outside world.

The first sales recorded by New Lebanon trustees were in 1789, leading one Shaker catalog from the nineteenth century to portray the Shakers as pioneers in the industry, possibly even the first to enter the business following the American Revolution. Shakers possibly sold a few other furnishings outside the community at times, but, with these isolated exceptions, they had only one true furniture commodity and that was chairs.

Shaker chairs came in all styles and sizes, from early single-slat, low-back dining chairs to tall four-slat rocking chairs to small children's chairs. No matter what the style, each chair reflected the Shakers' spiritual quest for perfection, for each one was meticulously crafted, pared-down and lightweight, strong and durable, and well-suited to fit the shape of the human body.

© Richard Day/Shakertown at South Union, KY

■ SHAKER FURNITURE CRAFTERS WERE AHEAD OF THEIR TIME, ANTICIPATING TODAY'S EMPHASIS ON ERGONOMICS BY DESIGNING CHAIRS TO FIT THE HUMAN BODIES FOR WHICH THEY WERE MADE, INCLUDING, OF COURSE, SPECIAL SMALL SEATING FOR CHILDREN.

Courtesy The Winterthur Library: The Edward Deming Andrews Memorial Shaker Collection

■ SLENDER, TALL CLOCKS ARE AN ESPECIALLY PRIZED SHAKER HANDIWORK. A SIMPLE DROP-LEAF TABLE DEMONSTRATES THE SHAKERS' VIGILANT EFFORT TO PRODUCE STREAMLINED HIGHLY EFFICIENT FURNITURE THAT TOOK UP MINIMAL SPACE.

▲ **THREE-SLAT LADDER-BACKS**   The most popular Shaker chair was the three-slat ladder-back, which, consequently, is the most readily available on today's market. The three back slats were bent slightly to round with the contours of the human back. Legs and back posts were gracefully turned on a lathe for a delicate look that was completed by round or pointed finials. Even the finials were not purely decorative but had utility, serving as handles. Belying the chairs' apparent fragility was a strength emanating from the construction of each post from a single piece of wood, with no parts screwed or glued on.

Back slats were commonly planed to a thickness of 5/16 of an inch (8 mm), and each successive slat was subtly graduated in width to accommodate the sitter comfortably. To economize on wood and weight, the Shakers gave their chairs the distinctive trait of legs which terminated with no feet. Legs were slightly tapered, also for the purpose of removing any unnecessary wood and lightening the weight. Tapering had the additional effect of imbuing each chair with a refined delicacy. This effortless elegance, even though the byproduct of function, gave the chairs an aesthetic superiority to anything contrived, and eliminated the need for ornamental painting or carving, gratuitous decoration shunned by the Shakers. The smooth wood, though, was anything but drab. Often it was finished to a bright yellow or red.

Chairs made for brethren are easily distinguished from those made for sisters, the brethren's chairs being larger. Beginning in 1793, brethren and sisters would line up their chairs in what were known as union meetings. These gatherings were held on the three evenings of the week when there were no religious services, and they were a part of the Shaker life for an entire century. An equal number of sisters and brethren would meet in a brother's retiring room, placing their chairs in rows "distant a few feet" apart from those of the opposite sex. In this manner, they discussed "any subject connected with their home and religious life"— the higher brethren chairs facing the lower sisters' chairs. After the dialogue ended, the Shaker separation acts once more applied: Brethren and sisters could not "go into each other's rooms after evening meetings" or even "talk together in the halls."

The ergonomic foresight of the Shakers was evidenced by their construction on the diagonal. By building chairs with a slight backward tilt, the Shakers ensured a better fit to the sitter's back.

The form-follows-function concept in furniture design is seen again in Shaker chairs' "tilter feet." Beginning in the mid-1800s, Shakers built chair backposts with wooden ball-and-socket tilter feet, which kept the back legs flat on the floor when the sitter tilted the chair backwards (a habit even the perfection-driven Shakers apparently could not break).

Courtesy The Winterthur Library: The Edward Deming Andrews Memorial Shaker Collection

The entire purpose behind this engineering feat was to prevent scuffing the soft pine floors, thus maintaining the Believers' high priority of meticulous cleanliness and order.

Until the mid-nineteenth century, the quality of Shaker chairs did not waver. Little difference in workmanship existed from the beginning of the century to the middle. With the advent of the Civil War, however, things changed. The Shakers were catering to a mass market and were relying, more and more, on timesaving machinery and more institutionalized routines. While the chairs retained the charms of simplicity and delicacy in appearance, with a

■ WHEN BELIEVERS MET AS A GROUP TO CONFER OUTSIDE OF WORSHIP, THEY LINED LADDER-BACK CHAIRS IN TWO ROWS FACING EACH OTHER—ONE FOR BRETHREN, THE OTHER FOR SISTERS.

Courtesy The Winterthur Library: The Edward Deming Andrews Memorial Shaker Collection

■ THE PURITY OF LINE IN SHAKER FURNITURE RESULTS IN ALMOST ANY GROUPING, SUCH AS THIS TRIPOD SEWING TABLE, CHAIR, AND INSPIRATIONAL DRAWING FROM HANCOCK, MASSACHUSETTS, EXUDING A LOOK THAT IS LYRICAL AND SERENE.

rugged underlying strength, certain details of production went unattended: Lathe marks were left visible instead of being sanded out; the mushroom-shaped turnings showed little individuality of design, but became standardized.

Interestingly, as the quality of their chairs suffered slightly with increased production, the Shakers' desire to protect their reputations rose. Sometime after 1852, when the New Lebanon chair industry was reorganized, the Shakers began marking their chairs with an applied gold transfer trademark that would distinguish authentic Shaker wares from derivative knockoffs trying to pose as Shaker.

Still, Shaker chairs were superior to the majority on the market. In 1876, at the Philadelphia Centennial, the Shaker entries won for their "strength, sprightliness and modest beauty." The Shakers themselves, in their *Centennial Illustrated Catalogue and Price List of the Shakers' Chairs*, issued in 1876 in Albany, wrote: "Our largest chairs do not weigh ten pounds, and the smallest weigh less than five pounds, and yet the largest person can feel safe in sitting down in them without fear of going through them."

▲ **TAPE SEATS**   One of the most distinctive traits of Shaker chairs is their colorful woven-tape seats, a Shaker invention that can be dated to as early as 1820. Prior to that, seats were woven with narrow hickory splints, and, later, with cane and rush. But once the Shakers hit on the idea of woven tapes, they preferred this seating treatment to the rest. Woven-tape seats had the advantages of being sturdy, comfortable, and easy to make. They had the added bonus of being vibrantly colored, giving the simple, straight-lined chairs an unexpected verve.

Seats were woven by Shaker sisters into herringbone and checkerboard patterns. The earliest tapes were made from the Shakers own yarns, which sisters spun and dyed themselves. Later, economics made it more sensible for the sisters to purchase twilled cotton tapes from outside, which they then wove by hand in the old manner. (Instructions for weaving a chair seat are found on page 72.)

The principle for weaving a seat was simple: Two layers of tape were carried over the wooden seat frame and woven together, with a layer of filling between them. The filler was a cloth pad filled with sawdust or horsehair. As the nineteenth century progressed, the tape more often was made of cotton than wool.

Weaving chairseats was the only contribution Shaker women made to the chairmaking industry, at least during its heyday, from the beginning to the middle of the nineteenth century. The Shaker society was based on equality, but separation, of the sexes. Elder Mary

Antoinette explained in 1880 that: "Woman was no longer a slave in bonds, forced as it were to bear down the name of some man to posterity, and bend over the cradle and sing lullaby as her only right, and the highest aim of her existence; but she became co-worker with her brother man in every department of life. Hence they stood shoulder to shoulder, each occupying their own sphere, yet working in harmonious relations together."

"Own sphere," then, meant that men did the carpentry, as well as the farming, stone-cutting, and other traditional male labors, while women did the sewing, which included weaving chairseats, as well as the cooking, cleaning, kitchen gardening, and laundering.

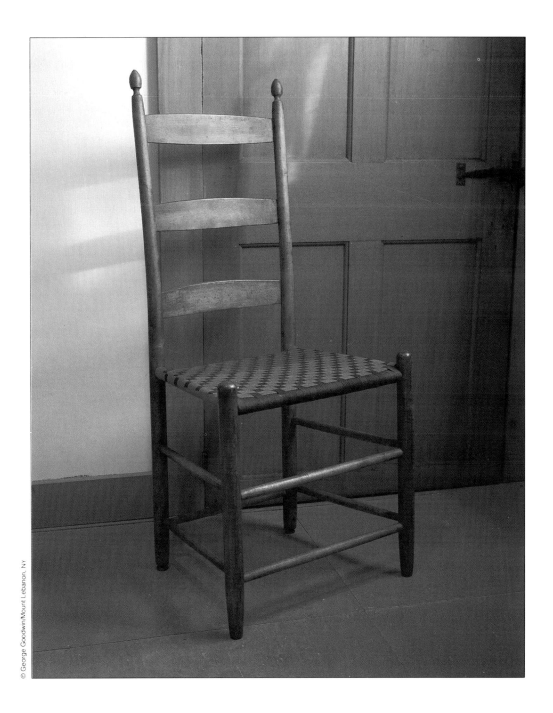

© George Goodwin/Mount Lebanon, NY

■ ALTHOUGH THE FURNITURE IS IMMINENTLY SIMPLISTIC AND UNADORNED, GRAPHIC BOLDNESS WAS IMPARTED ON THE CHECKERBOARD WEAVE OF THE CHAIR'S TAPE SEAT.

Courtesy The Winterthur Library: The Edward Deming Andrews Memorial Shaker Collection

■ *ABOVE:* TAPING CHAIR SEATS FELL WITHIN SISTERS' DOMAIN. SISTER SARAH COLLINS (1855-1947) OF NEW LEBANON, NEW YORK, IS SHOWN HERE DEMONSTRATING THE WEAVING PROCESS. *ABOVE, RIGHT:* MORE UNUSUAL SHAKER CHAIRS INCLUDE TAPE BACK AND FOUR-SLAT BACK ROCKERS.

© Richard Day/Shakertown at South Union, KY

The conventional distribution of the work load probably was a matter of tacit mutual consent, brethren and sisters being content to pursue that which they knew best. The separation of work, though, was set down officially by Millennial Laws: "Brethren and sisters' shops, should not be under one and the same roof, except those of the Ministry."

While men were crafting chairs in the cabinet shops, women were spinning the fibers into yarns for tapes in their own spinning shops, then weaving the chairseats, in total segregation from the men.

There is some evidence, however, that that may have changed as operations became more mechanized. Later chairs are documented as having not only their tape seats made by a sister, but also the bodies. Sister Lillian Barlow is one Shaker woman credited with woodworking skills. Circa-1924 production chairs have been attributed to her, as have circa-1900 to 1930 production rocking chairs, whose seats were taped by Sister Sarah Collins.

▲ **REVOLVERS** Shakers were inventors par excellence. Because of the anonymity of the individual inventor, and the Shakers' hesitancy to seek patents (which they believed signified a monopoly—an idea in direct opposition to communal ownership), they are not given the recognition they deserve. A distinctive chair of Shaker invention, and one that has remained popular ever since, is the revolving chair. Both revolving chairs and swivel stools were widely produced by the Shakers, and in many sizes and styles, according to need. They were especially popular as sewing chairs. Some were used as piano stools, while taller ones functioned well for the needs of bank tellers and accountants.

In their inventory, the Shakers recorded these rotating action chairs as "revolvers." This made at least one curator nonplussed, wondering why the pacifistic Shakers, who were staunchly opposed to bearing arms and who refused to fight in any battle, including the Civil War, were in the business of manufacturing weapons. Finally, the confusion dissipated when the revolver was identified as a chair, not a firearm.

▲ **ROCKERS**   The Shakers cannot lay claim to inventing the rocking chair, but they were among the first in America to outfit chairs with rockers and to do so in any significant number. Initially, Shaker rocking chairs were crafted only for elderly and infirm brethren and sisters. Eventually, though, rocking chairs became standard furniture assigned to retiring rooms in Shaker dwellings.

At New Lebanon, which was the hub of the Shaker chairmaking industry, no chairs outfitted with rockers were known to have been made before 1800. From 1805 to 1807, more than three hundred chairs were produced, but only three of those were rocking chairs.

Shaker rocking chairs can be loosely grouped into five different styles: the mushroom post, which had turnings shaped like a mushroom at the top of the front leg tenons; the scrolled arm; rolled arm; cushion-rail; and sewing rocker. Most of the early rockers were included in the first three groups, and all showed the influences of colonial craftsmanship, with no radically innovative designs. All of the chairs had four back slats, two rungs in the front and one in the rear, and low arms. Slats on the early rocking chairs were secured by hand-chiseled, irregular square dowels. On later chairs, only the top slat was doweled.

Towards the mid-1800s, an increasing awareness of comfort resulted in the advent of the cushion-rail chair. This was made similarly to the four-slat rocking chair, except that a curved rod above the top slat connected the two back posts. The rod's purpose was for hanging a plush mat to provide softer sitting.

The shift away from strict asceticism towards greater comfort was not without its detractors. The rocking chair became something of a sitting duck for attacks from the more traditional, hard-line Shakers. On April 11, 1840, in a message delivered to the ministry and elders at New Lebanon, one Believer, Philemon Stewart, questioned, "How comes it about that there are so many rocking chairs used? Is the rising generation going to be able to keep the way of God, by seeking after ease?"

Courtesy The Winterthur Library: Tre Edward Deming Andrews Memorial Shaker Collection

■ THE GRACEFUL LINES OF A SHAKER ROCKING CHAIR AND TRIPOD TABLE ARE ECHOED IN A PIPE RACK.

Courtesy The Winterthur Library: The Edward Deming Andrews Memorial Shaker Collection

■ LONG, SPINDLE-BACK BENCHES WERE FAVORED FOR THE MUSIC ROOM AT CANTERBURY, NEW HAMPSHIRE.

▲ **BENCHES**   Even before they began building chairs, the Shakers were crafting benches to meet their seating needs. It was benches, not slat-back chairs, that first flanked trestle tables in the dining halls of the early Shaker communities. The appearance of Shaker-made benches can be traced to the time the first communities were founded. Chairs were scarce then, and communal living demanded a large number of seatings at mealtime. Long, rudimentary benches provided the solution.

Benches also solved a seating problem in the early communities' meetinghouses. Their use there, however, proved so satisfactory that they continued to be used until the close of the nineteenth century.

The standard appearance of a meetinghouse bench was ten feet (3 m) long and sixteen inches (40 cm) high. These long benches were used during worship services for both Believers and visitors. The simplest New Lebanon bench had a sturdy plank stretched atop two or three legs, whose bases were cut into arched shapes. The legs were braced with small wood pieces that were half-dovetailed into an edge of the plank.

One of the best-known Shaker benches is the Canterbury bench, named after the Canterbury settlement from which it presumably hails. (Some speculation holds the bench as originating in the Harvard community.) Used in meetinghouses, the Canterbury bench was made as early as 1855. Its construction featured a back of numerous vertical spindles that supported a shaped, horizontal back rest. The seat consisted of a single slab of wood. Much more elegant than the plain, backless New Lebanon bench, the Canterbury bench also was reasonably comfortable, due to its shaping and sound proportions.

▲ TRESTLE TABLES

Occasionally Shaker tables were sold outside the community, but largely they were designed for internal use only. Consequently, they were not as standardized as Shaker chairs, which had to follow a more rigid design model for quantity production.

The favorite dining table for communal living was the trestle style. Having no obstructions underfoot, this table could seat the maximum number of persons and provide the greatest amount of legroom.

Unlike the early-American trestle table, the Shaker version was much lighter. To increase legroom, it lacked the colonial trestle's center rail, which was placed halfway down the leg; instead, Shaker trestle tables were connected just below the top, where there would be no spatial interference.

© MacDonald Photography/Envision/Hancock Shaker Village, MA

■ FOR COMMUNAL LIVING, PLAIN BANQUET TABLES AND STURDY CHAIRS SUFFICED FOR DINING.

Early trestle tables were extremely simple, consisting of chamfered posts and tapered, flat feet. Later versions featured arched feet and posts that were either scrolled or turned. The simplicity of both early and later models would have pleased Mother Ann, who condemned possession of "costly and extravagant furniture" as nothing short of sin. Upon visiting one home, she insisted that its occupants "never put on silver spoons for me nor tablecloths, but let your tables be clean enough to eat on without cloths; and if you do not know what to do with them, give them to the poor."

According to the Shaker separation acts for the sexes, a brother and sister could not "eat at one table, unless there is company"—just as they could not "ride together in a wagon without company" or even "be in a room together without company." The standard routine had brethren occupying one table and sisters, another.

Tabletops usually were made out of pine, while an assortment of other woods—including ash, maple, walnut, cherry, and oak—were used for the rest of the table body. Ministry tables, which were shorter than the communal dining tables (communal tables typically measured ten feet [3m] by three feet [1m] with some spanning as much as twenty feet [6m] in length), sometimes were constructed entirely out of cherry, or, in the western communities, entirely of walnut.

▲ FOUR-LEGGED TABLES AND TRIPODS

Shakers made four-legged tables in every conceivable size, style, and wood. Many were designed for specific tasks—the drop-leaf sewing table, for instance, or an elongated table, which facilitated one of the Shakers' many industries.

Expressing their utility, some of the tables featured staggered apron drawers, which made it easy for two or more Believers to work at the table at the same time.

For the heavier shop chores and kitchen tasks, some of the four-legged tables were more massive than typical Shaker furniture. Bread-cutting tables, for example, consisted of an unusually heavy square top on splayed legs. These tables were highly functional laborsavers: At one side or in the center of the top there was a long-handled knife that swung on a pivot for the speedy slicing of bread loaves.

Even the most ungainly (by Shaker standards) of these practical furnishings met with the approval of Elder Frederick Evans, one of the Believers' primary spokespersons: "The beautiful . . . has no business with us. The divine man has no right to waste money upon what you people would call beauty, in his house or his daily life, while there are people living in misery," he said.

© Richard Day/The Kentucky Museum Collection, Western Kentucky University

© Richard Day/The Kentucky Museum Collection, Western Kentucky University

■ HIGHLY FUNCTIONAL SEWING TABLES *(ABOVE, LEFT)* AND TRIPODS *(ABOVE, RIGHT)*—BOTH SHOWN HERE ARE C.1850—ARE AMONG THE MOST ETHEREAL OF SHAKER FURNISHINGS.

Despite their diversity, the four-legged Shaker tables featured one of two types of leg—either square and tapered, or plain and turned. Those used as nightstands, chairtables, or sofa end tables by today's collectors were pared down to a perfectly proportioned, lightweight, essential form.

In addition to four-legged tables, the Shakers crafted tripods—three-legged table-size pedestals, which were made in either a refined or utilitarian style. The working tripods were designed in a plethora of styles for varied purposes. Some were used for reading stands, while others functioned as sewing or seed-sorting pedestals. They were usually constructed with pegged, unadorned chamfered legs.

Contrasting with the working tripods was a more elegant version. Usually made of cherry, these round-top pedestals were gracefully turned and were a part of most retiring rooms. They serve as stellar examples of the Shakers' exquisite craftsmanship, and, in truth, are art.

Courtesy The Henry Francis du Pont Winterthur Museum

■ NEARLY EVERY ROOM IN A SHAKER DWELLING FEATURED ENTIRE WALLS OR PORTIONS OF WALLS WITH BUILT-IN DRAWERS, CABINETS, AND SHELVES, FACILITATING THE COMMUNAL LIFESTYLE BY OFFERING THE EASY STORAGE EVERYONE IN THE COMMUNITY WAS FAMILIAR WITH.

▲ BUILT-IN CUPBOARDS AND DRAWERS

Shaker furniture and architecture were compatible, each serving to reinforce and meld with the other. The division between them narrowed even further when the furniture was built-in. The built-in cupboards and drawers, which were such an integral part of the Shaker community, functioned and were constructed as furniture, but their fixed position in the wall made them as much an architectural feature as a furnishing.

Built-in furnishings were emblematic of nearly every building in a Shaker community. Illustrating their pervasiveness, a single room in a dwelling in Enfield, New Hampshire, had 860 drawers built into its walls—and that is in addition to built-in cupboards, which also graced the space.

Built-ins were usually made from pine and butternut. They were made entirely of wood, including drawer and cabinet pulls.

Like all other Shaker furnishings, built-ins served specific purposes. Part of a wall at the Hancock community, for instance, included eighty-four built-in, numbered drawers of varying sizes for the storage of herbs. Similarly, other Shaker shops for specialized enterprises had built-ins geared to the needs of their particular industry.

Like portable Shaker furnishings, built-ins were carefully crafted. Drawers featured the same precise dovetailing and attention to detail. The finished product generally was painted Shaker blue or mustard yellow.

▲ DESKS

The Shakers crafted desks for two groups within their community of Believers: schoolchildren and the ministry. Except for the purpose of maintaining scrupulous business records on the day-to-day operations of the community, Shakerism frowned on writing for any other purpose. From the Shaker standpoint, writing was the epitome of vanity—an act of self-perpetuation and self-absorption completely at odds with the communal lifestyle.

In the 1821 Millennial Laws, it was specifically decreed: "Writing desks may not be used by common members, unless they have much public writing to do. But writing desks may be used as far as it is thought proper by the lead."

The average adult, then, seldom had access to a writing desk.

▲ ADULT DESKS

A vast assortment of desk styles were produced, however, for those elders in a community whose positions of leadership required them to keep records and inventories.

One style was the portable laptop. These were the paradigms of order—a place for everything, including ink bottles, pens, and papers, all neatly compartmentalized beneath a slant-top lid. Laptop desks, it is believed, were of particular value when the members of the ministry were required to leave their own community to travel to another settlement of Believers—visits which, considering the level of communication between the various groups, were not infrequent.

© Richard Day/Shakertown at South Union, KY

■ SHAKER DESKS ARE RARE, RESULTING FROM BELIEVERS' CONVICTION THAT WRITING FOR ITS OWN SAKE IS SELF-SERVING NARCISSISM. ADULT DESKS WERE CREATED PRIMARILY FOR TRUSTEES, WHO REQUIRED THEM FOR KEEPING COMMUNITY BOOKS AND RECORDS.

Four-legged desks, for the most part, were constructed as slant-lidded desks with legs. There is little repetition or standardization of size, which could be evidence that nearly every desk was custom-designed to fit the size of a particular individual. A few of the desks featured especially graceful tapered legs, indicating, perhaps, their construction as gifts for favorite elders.

In addition to the slant-top desk, the Shakers also produced what would be known today as a secretary—a cupboard with a drop-lid writing surface. An even more unusual style was a chest of drawers in which one drawer dropped open, into a desk. This kind of concealed dual function was extremely rare, though, in a society that favored total honesty and lack of pretense or duplicity.

Another style of desk was for sewing. Flat-topped, the sewing desk was outfitted with slots and drawers for storing spools of thread, scissors, and other materials. Some were made with drawers on the side, to prevent the user from having to bend beneath the desktop for materials—another example of the Shakers' innovative functionalism.

A sewing desk was the first Shaker furnishing to be sold at public auction in the 1990s. A double desk, built to accommodate two users at the same time, it was considered a bargain at the going bid of $33,000. Made of butternut, pine, birch, and cherry, the forty-four-inch (112-cm) desk bears the signature of "B.H. Smith 1862"—a fact that was not known until after the auction and would probably have raised the bidding.

Other woods commonly used to build desks were oak and maple. Western Shaker communities created more ornate varieties, with the tops circumscribed by a row of spindles.

▲ **SCHOOL DESKS** Schoolchildren's desks were a crude form of the adult slant-top desk. Census records show that the early communities included large numbers of children: For example, in 1813, South Union, Kentucky, had 164 adults and 143 children—the latter of which all had to be educated. As communities matured, the population of children fell considerably. But starting out, developing a system of schooling was a major concern. Elder Molly Goodrich once complained of the South Union children that "many are too young to learn their books."

School-age children usually lived in special structures, apart from the dwelling houses of adults. At South Union, their studies were first divided into semesters by gender and workload, with boys attending school three months in the late fall and winter, and girls scheduled for three months in the early spring. By getting schoolwork out of the way during these slack months, the children were free to help with the pressing chores and busy seasons.

Subject matter covered only the basics: reading, writing, arithmetic, geography, and spelling. Letter writing was also a part of the curriculum, making the need for appropriate desks particularly urgent.

The slow development of public schools resulted in many non-Believers sending their children to Shaker schools on a paid tuition basis. The large number of Believers' children, plus the attendance of children from "the world," necessitated a relatively large number of school desks.

But even for children, desks were strictly utilitarian: a bare-bones necessity for a bare-bones education. For the Shakers, a child's education years were not a time for pampering or coddling to ensure proper development of the mind; accordingly, the accoutrements of education, desks, were provided in their most rudimentary form.

New Lebanon Elder Seth Y. Wells who, with Elder Calvin Green, wrote *A Summary View of the Millennial Church* in 1823, observed that: "This life is short at the longest, and ought not to be spent in acquiring any kind of knowledge which can not be put to good use." The Shaker education system was not aimed at producing scholars but only at equipping students with "as much letter learning as may be put to proper use, and fit them for business in the Society of Believers . . . to give proper exercise to their mental faculties, & turn those faculties into the proper channel of usefulness for their own benefit & the benefit of their Brethren & Sisters."

© Richard Day/Shakertown at South Union, KY

■ ANOTHER EXCEPTION TO THE SHAKERS' DISLIKES WAS IN RELATION TO CHILDREN. EDUCATION OF CHILDREN WAS TAKEN SERIOUSLY BY BELIEVERS , AND SCHOOL DESKS WERE PROVIDED FOR THEM.

Courtesy The Winterthur Library: The Edward Deming Andrews Memorial Shaker Collection

■ A COLLECTION OF CANDLESTANDS FROM NEW LEBANON, NEW YORK, ILLUSTRATE THE DIVERSITY OF DESIGNS EMPLOYED, EVEN BY A SINGLE COMMUNITY, IN CREATING A SINGLE PRODUCT.

▲ OTHER FURNISHINGS

Because of their strict adherence to a doctrine of cleanliness, the Shakers required washstands as a staple furnishing. Probably one washstand was allocated to each retiring room, and certainly they were included in the communal washrooms.

Mirrors, on the other hand, while important for confirming one's grooming, were not considered essentials. To discourage vanity, they were kept small—none were to exceed twelve inches (30 cm) by eighteen inches (45 cm).

Case furniture, specifically chests of drawers, were rare in Shaker communities prior to 1800. Lift-top blanket chests appeared a little earlier, probably around 1790. In addition to the Shakers' built-in drawers and cupboards, though, chests were in great demand in keeping with the idea of "a place for everything and everything in its place." When not in use, all clothing and bedclothes were neatly stored from view, dust, and dirt. Clothing, discreetly bearing its wearer's initials, was folded in chests when not hung in one of the communal cupboards.

Unlike most Shaker furnishings, chests were often signed by their cabinetmakers—usually beneath one of the drawer panels.

The earliest lift-top blanket chests, also called "six board chests," were made of white pine that was painted a dark red. As the chests evolved, they included first one, two, and then three drawers.

Occasionally, a chest of drawers included a lock (some children's chests are known examples), but this was a rare exception. In the "Orders and Rules and Counsels for the People of God" issued in 1841, it was mandated that Believers "shall not lock, nor fasten by secret means, nor cause it to be done, any cupboard, drawer, chest, or writing box belonging to any individual." Millennial Laws further stated that "no private possession should be kept under lock and key security, without liberty from the Elders . . . . It is desirable to have all so trustworthy that locks and keys will be needless." God's people were to be presumed innocent and blameless; locks challenged that and, therefore, were discouraged.

© Jeanetta Ho/Dunham Tavern Museum Collection

■ IT WAS MANDATED IN 1841 THAT SHAKER CHESTS "SHALL NOT LOCK, NOR FASTEN BY SECRET MEANS" BECAUSE SUCH PRECAUTIONS FOR SECURITY WOULD IMPLY DISTRUST IN A COMMUNITY OF BELIEVERS FOUNDED AND BOUND BY HONESTY.

■ *ABOVE:* SOFTENED BY QUILTS AND HOMEY ACCESSORIES, SHAKER FURNISHINGS MELD NICELY INTO A WARM COUNTRY STYLE. *OPPOSITE PAGE:* THE STRONG LINES OF SHAKER PIECES IMBUE A ROOM WITH A POWERFUL PRESENCE.

▲ **SPIRIT OF SHAKER** A single Shaker furnishing imparts a distinctive quality—a simple beauty—to a room. However, outfitting an entire home in authentic Shaker pieces is another matter.

The problem isn't whether or not the home will succeed as an aesthetically pleasing living environment. Assuredly it will, since Shaker furniture fits well into any decor. The problem is whether dressing a home, head to toe, in this manner is within the owner's means.

Shaker furnishings are not inexpensive. Trying to keep track of their usually steady, sometimes mercurial, and often inexplicable increases in value is a losing proposition. Even the most current auction catalog quickly is dated.

A more realistic approach—and one that the ever-pragmatic Shakers themselves most likely would applaud—is to combine carefully chosen Shaker collections with other furnishings or accessories that are less costly and more comfortable for today's lifestyle. There is also a second alternative: to attain the Shaker design aesthetic, not through vintage Shaker pieces at all, but through Shaker reproductions, which replicate the style, proportions, and materials of authentic Shaker antiques, but without the history and pricetag of genuine Shaker craftsmanship.

▲ **BLENDED STYLE** The first option—blending authentic Shaker pieces within the context of other room furnishings—has several attractive features. First, limiting the number of Shaker furnishings in your home enables you to collect only outstanding pieces. Another practical implication of melding Shaker with other decorating styles is comfort. Let's face it: The enveloping physical comfort of a down-filled sofa or an overstuffed armchair is not to be found in the Shaker oeuvre.

In a living room designed with comfortable seating, the addition of a Shaker chair can add welcoming geometry and be a key element in an artistic vignette. An antique taped Shaker chair showcased against a clean white wall allows form, balance, and finish to make an impact on a room otherwise lacking in crisp, definitive linear character. Because Shaker furniture is constructed entirely of wood, its juxtaposition in a room with upholstered pieces provides visual contrast between hard and soft, adding interest to the space.

Shaker furnishings aren't limited to blending in with any single style. They work well in colonial settings, from which their own forms hail, but they also are warm additions to more eclectic country decors and even to slick, minimalistic contemporary interiors. The bold checks of a pair of Shaker taped-seat chairs, for example, may be just the jolt of color a monochromatic modern room needs.

Courtesy Yield House, Inc.

■ REPRODUCTION SHAKER FURNISHINGS, SUCH AS THIS CUPBOARD FROM YIELD HOUSE, PROVIDE AN ALTERNATIVE FOR THE SHAKER ADMIRER WHO FINDS ANTIQUE PRICES PROHIBITIVE.

Shaker additions don't even have to be furniture. Shaker accessories can charge a space with warmth and character. An old country cupboard, for example, becomes the focal point of a dining room and pièce de résistance when filled with a collection of Shaker oval boxes and wooden carriers of varying sizes and finishes.

▲ REPRODUCTION STYLE

It takes a while to amass a Shaker collection, even when the goal is considerably short of filling an entire house. For the Shaker aficionado not in a position to stalk the vanishing supply of Shaker furnishings at auctions and shops around the country, there is good news. Beautifully reproduced Shaker furniture is available as an alternative.

Reproductions usually mean that handcrafted items are made by a single cabinetmaker working alone in a studio or shop. Geographical distances between these small shops and consumers isn't the barrier it might be. Most Shaker reproduction craftspersons produce catalogs or brochures of their work, accompanied by price lists, and most will ship their products to the buyer. Check the source listing beginning on page 154 for shops to contact for reproduction furniture.

Although the Shaker purist might flinch at the thought of buying new Shaker-style furniture, there are advantages. In addition to a lower cost, reproductions are much more widely available. As the rarified world of Shaker antiques narrows, the circle of reproductions expands. Purchasing reproductions doesn't require the extensive search finding an antique can entail. These finds are only a catalog's inventory away.

▲ COLLECTING

As with any specialized antique, for authenticity and buyer satisfaction to be assured Shaker furnishings must be approached with a respect approaching wariness. The Shaker market is subject to its fair share of fraudulence, with knockoffs—reproductions posing as the originals—infiltrating all areas. Even ephemeral—a category of collectibles encompassing Shaker printed paper items such as seed packets and advertisements—are host to a rash of fakery. For the neophyte collector, the adage "buyer beware" is less a cliche than a wise admonition.

Seasoned antiquers only just venturing into the province of Shaker already know how to best safeguard against bad purchases: Do your homework. Research. Read books on Shaker furniture. Study the photographs carefully, developing an eye for proportion and construction. Study the details. Now, more than ever, there is good resource material on the market to introduce you to, and educate you about, the world of Shaker.

But books alone aren t enough. Nothing can replace firsthand observation. Go to Shaker villages and museums and take the time to look. This contact won't be as hands-on as you might like, however, because most of the pieces can't be touched, thus precluding too close an examination.

After viewing authentic Shaker pieces in their natural environment, find a reputable dealer who specializes in Shaker articles. Visit, examine, ask questions. There is probably a reason one Shaker chair is priced higher than another that, to the uninitiated eye, appears to be identical. More than likely, the dealer will explain that the more expensive chair is entirely original, while the less costly one may have been extensively restored or has had many repairs. Although the repairs may be virtually undetectable and you decide you want the lower-priced chair despite them, you should at least be aware of what you are getting. Be an informed buyer, not an ignorant buyer.

Buying from the power-seat of knowledge is particularly important at auction, where it can be easy to make costly mistakes. Consult the auction catalog prior to the event. Compare pieces to be auctioned with those in your reference books to determine their quality. Set a limit on what you are willing to spend.

Prices for Shaker pieces, as with any other antique, will be based on condition, amount of repair, finish (original paint or finish increases value), rarity, form, size, style, age, and signature or other identifying mark.

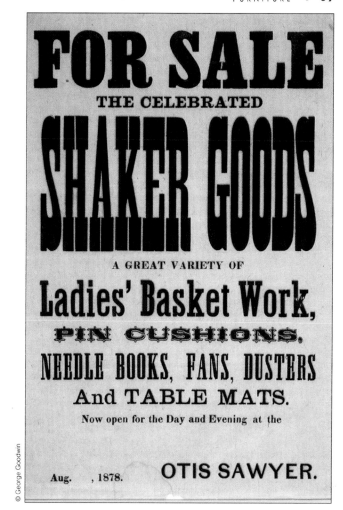

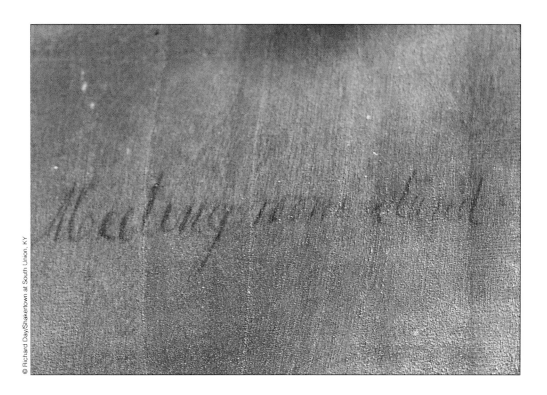

■ *Above:* Merchants recognized the popularity of the high-quality Shaker goods, and they advertised accordingly. *Left:* Prices of Shaker antiques increase when identifying marks or signs are present, such as this inscription on the bottom of a tall candlestand from South Union, Kentucky.

■ *RIGHT:* OVAL BOXES AND SEWING CARRIERS ARE AMONG THE MOST POPULAR SHAKER COLLECTIBLES. *OPPOSITE PAGE:* WHEN BOTH FURNISHINGS AND ARCHITECTURE ARE SHAKER, ROOMS TAKE ON A BOLD, LINEAR CHARACTER.

© Philip M. Zito/Dunham Tavern Museum Collection

▲ **EVALUATING SHAKER PIECES** There are some other specific criteria to look for when you are planning on buying Shaker furniture and other Shaker collectibles:

▲ Oval sewing carriers or other wooden sewing accessories made at Sabbathday Lake have their village's trademark stamped on the bottom in black ink.

▲ Oval boxes, practical collectibles thanks to their small size and easy identification as Shaker, should feature delicately carved fingers, perfectly aligned vertical tacks, freedom from cracks, and a pleasing oval shape.

▲ Non-production chairs will have more classic styling and proportions than those produced later (made for mass market) and will bear higher prices.

▲ Case furniture is most difficult to identify as Shaker and requires the greatest degree of knowledge on the part of the buyer. Much of it was based on eighteenth-century Sheraton, Hepplewhite, Queen Anne, and other prevailing styles, and therefore features similarities. Wood is an invaluable clue here. Know the woods indigenous to each Shaker community—if a piece claiming to be from a Shaker village is made of a wood not associated with that community, shy away from purchasing it—or, at least, double-check its provenance. Research into the kinds of nails, screws, and hardware used at various times by the Shaker cabinetmakers is also important in helping to identify a piece.

© Brian Vanden Brink/Sabbathday Lake, ME

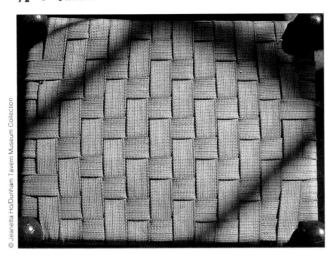

© Jearetta Ho/Dunham Tavern Museum Collection

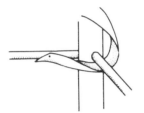

▲ FIG. 1

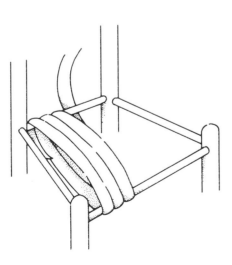

▲ FIG. 2

TAPE WEAVING SHAKER CHAIRS
▲▲▲

THE FOLLOWING INSTRUCTIONS ARE EXCERPTED FROM *CHAIR SEAT WEAVING FOR ANTIQUE CHAIRS*, DISTRIBUTED BY CONNECTICUT CANE AND REED CO.

If you can't find a genuine Shaker chair for your tape weaving, or feel that you can't afford one, get a good substitute and indulge yourself in the fun of weaving a cloth seat.

You will be making a double seat, weaving the same pattern on both the top and bottom of the chair. This can be done either standing at a table or sitting down.

The only tools you need can be found at home: scissors, a dinner knife or narrow steel spatula, a hammer, and tacks. Needle and thread may also be required.

To prepare the chair for tape weaving, glue the joints if they are loose and refinish the chair to the natural wood. Fill in any irregularities on the chair rails and sand them smooth, if necessary.

▲ MATERIALS

▲ 2 YARDS (1.8 M) CLOSELY WOVEN DARK COTTON CLOTH

▲ 34 INCHES (85 CM) OF 1-INCH- (2.5-CM-) THICK TAPE OR 40 INCHES (1 M) OF 5/8-OF-AN-INCH- (1.5- CM-)-THICK TAPE

Before ordering tape, it is advisable to send the measurements of your chair to the seat-weaving supply house and they will send you the right amount of tape. It comes in two widths and a variety of colors. The Shakers always used contrasting colors and were fond of red and black in a checkerboard pattern.

▲ STUFFING

To make the stuffing, cut one piece of cloth that will fit the shape of the chair seat and will have four flaps cut a little shorter than the four rails. These flaps are glued to the rails, and hold the pillow in place. For the top of the pillow, cut a piece of cloth smaller than the size of the seat and stitch to the bottom piece. Stuff the pillow so that it is two to three inches (5 to 8 cm) thick. Fasten it to the chair rails by gluing the flaps around the rails on all four sides. Let dry thoroughly.

▲ TAPING THE CHAIR

▲ STEP 1: WARPING   The tape seat is a double seat with the same weaving on the underside as on the top of the seat. The tabby weave is the most common weave used by the Shakers. It is woven from one side of the chair to the other, and under and over the warp strips, securely locking the warp strips in place.

To put the warp strips on the chair, take the coil of tape to be used for the warp and tack the end firmly to the inner side of the left rail in front of the left back post (fig. 1). Bring the tape under the back rail next to the left back post, over it, and to the front rail in a straight line. The tape must be at right angles to the front rail. Take the tape over and around the front rail, under and over the back rail, and continue in this manner until you reach the right back post (fig. 2). You are wrapping the front and back rails with tape to make a double seat. All the warp strips must be at right angles to the front rail with a little slack to them.

When you finish at the front rail and have no room for another warp on the back rail, bring the tape under the front rail and to the back right post, allow two extra inches (5 cm) of tape and cut the rest off (fig. 3). Tack this end of the warp temporarily to the right side rail on the underside. You will weave it into the weft when you start the pattern weave.

▲ STEP 2: PATTERN WEAVING   Pattern weaving is done with the weft tape, which is also referred to as the weaver. Cut off about ten yards (9 m) of tape, less if you feel this is too much to handle easily, and turn your chair to the bottom side to start your first row of tabby, the pattern weave (fig. 4).

With the end of the tape, start at the left back post, go over the first warp strip, under the next one, over one, under one, until you reach the right back post of the chair (fig. 5). Pull the weaver through the warp strips, leaving an end of about two inches (5 cm), which can be folded under the first warp. It can be tacked to the underside if you wish, but it is not necessary.

Turn the chair right side up and bring the weaver around the right side rail, weaving over the first warp, under the next, over one, and continue across the chair. Pull the tape through and let this row curve to the back rail a little in order to hold the warp strips in place.

For the second row on the underside of the chair, weave under the first warp, over the next, doing just the opposite of what you did in weaving the first row. When you finish this row push the tape close to the previous row. On the top of the chair seat, weave in the same manner, pushing the row close to the first one.

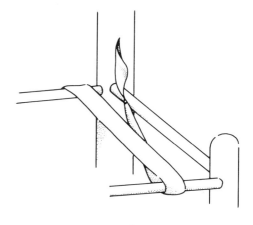

▲ FIG. 3

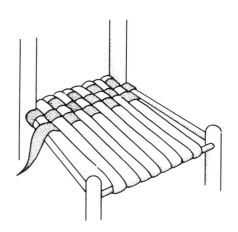

▲ FIG. 4

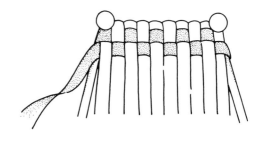

▲ FIG. 5

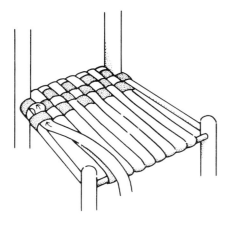

▲ FIG. 6

You now have two rows of weaving on the top and bottom of the chair seat. You will notice that the side rails of the chair are at an angle and flare out to meet the upright posts on either side of the wider front rail. You have a space without warps on the front rail beside the posts and a space along the side rails, triangular in shape, with no warps. These spaces are to be filled with added warps (short lengths of the warping tape) that are woven into the weft to fill the spaces.

▲ STEP 3: FILLING IN THE CORNERS   With two rows of pattern weaving done, turn the chair to the underside, untack the end of the warping if you finished at the front rail, and weave it into the weft in front of the right back post folding the end under (fig. 6).

On the top of the chair two warps can now be added in front of the two back posts. Measure two lengths of the warping tape that are double the length of the chair seat from front to back, add five inches (13 cm) for folding the ends under the weft, and cut off. Weave them into the top and bottom of the chair seat, making sure that they follow the pattern of the rest of the weaving. The right warp strip will have to wait to be woven into the weft if the warping ended on the front rail and its end is already woven in front of the right back post on the underside. In a few more rows of weft weaving there will be room to weave in the right strip along the side rail.

There may be no need for any more warp strips along the side rails of the chair, but if there is still space on the front rail to be filled, more warp strips can be added as the weaving progresses. If there is a space too small for another warp strip along the front rail next to the posts, leave it. Never overlap the warp strips.

As the weaving progresses to the front of the chair it is time to check the rows of warp and weft. As the warp strips are loose they tend to move out of position. Use a right angle of cardboard to see that they are all at right angles to the front rail. A straight edge will serve to check the rows of weft, since it is hard to keep them straight. If you can do this, the tabby weave will look much better.

On the last few rows at the front of the chair the warp strips will be hard to raise to allow the weft to pass under them. I have found the best help to be a dinner knife. Fold the end of the weaver over the tip of the knife and slide the knife under the warp strip. Any narrow piece of metal that is smooth and thin will serve the same purpose.

The last row on top of the chair will be next to the front posts on the side rails and should curve a little to the front rail to keep the warps smooth and flat. If there is no room to weave this last row, let the tape follow the last pattern row and end at the center.

▲ JOINING

To join a new length of tape to the weft simply overlap the new and old ends, hiding the end of the new tape under a warp. Always join a new tape to the old tape in the center of the underside, even though this means cutting off some of the tape to make the addition come in the right place, then sew together.

Courtesy The Winterthur Library: The Edward Deming Andrews Memorial Shaker Collection

BRAIDED RAG RUG
▲▲▲

▲ MATERIALS

- ▲ 5 POUNDS OF RAGS, PREFERABLY WOOL OR COTTON
- ▲ TAILOR'S CHALK
- ▲ YARDSTICK
- ▲ SHARP SCISSORS
- ▲ IRON
- ▲ SEWING MACHINE
- ▲ NEEDLE
- ▲ LINEN THREAD

▲ STEP 1: Remove lining and non-material parts of the fabric and cut the rags along the seams. Wash the rags in hot water.

▲ STEP 2: Mark 2½-inch-wide-strips of fabric with tailor's chalk, using the yardstick as a guide. Cut strips along the grain of the fabric.

▲ STEP 3: Stitch the strip together on a sewing machine on the bias by placing the end of one strip on top of and perpendicular to the other (fig. 1).

▲ STEP 4: Trim seams to ¼ inch; press open (figs. 2 and 3).

▲ STEP 5: Fold the outer edges of each strip toward the center, so the edges meet (fig. 4). Then fold the strip again so the folded edges meet, creating four thicknesses of fabric (fig. 5). Steam press to set the folds. Roll each folded strip around itself to form a wheel.

▲ STEP 6: Sew two separate strips together as you did above: Place one strip on top of and perpendicular to the other, then stitch on the bias (fig. 6). Lay the joined strips flat; place the end of a third strip between the fold of the first two to make a T-shape (fig. 7). As you braid, always keep the open edges of each strip to the left.

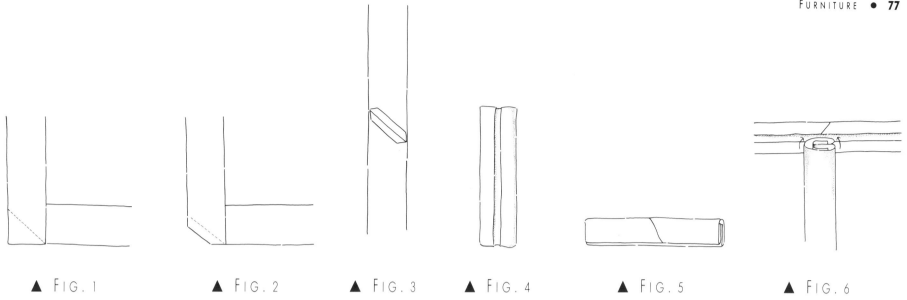

▲ FIG. 1   ▲ FIG. 2   ▲ FIG. 3   ▲ FIG. 4   ▲ FIG. 5   ▲ FIG. 6

▲ FIG. 7   ▲ FIG. 7A   ▲ FIG. 7B   ▲ FIG. 8

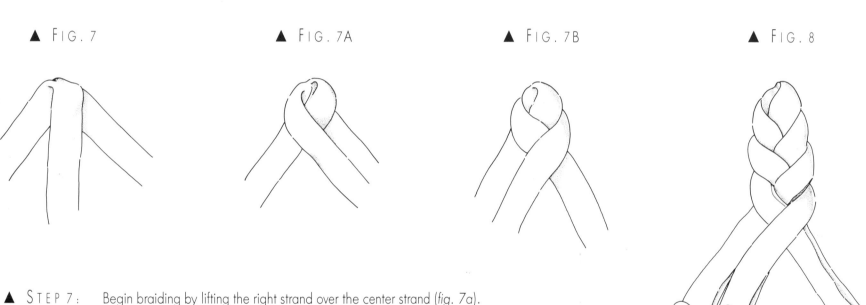

▲ STEP 7:   Begin braiding by lifting the right strand over the center strand (fig. 7a). Then lift the left strand over the new center strand. Continue like this, keeping an even tension, but without stretching the braid. Stitch new strips to the working strips as necessary and continue braiding (fig. 7b).

▲ STEP 8:   Sew the braids together using heavy thread and a strong needle. Beginning at the center, insert the needle into a space on the rug with an upward stroke, then pick up the loop on the braid with a downward stroke. Sewing it this way interlocks the braid instead of just stitching it side by side. Your next upstroke picks up the adjacent strand of the adjacent braid. Stitch every loop except on curves, where you should skip every other loop.

© Philip M. Zito

Chapter Three

▲▲▲

CLOTHING AND
TEXTILES

"Tis a gift to be simple."

TRADITIONAL SHAKER HYMN

North Wind Picture Archives

■ SHAKERS AT A SINGING MEETING AT NEW LEBANON, NEW YORK, ARE SHOWN IN CLOTHING THAT WAS TYPICAL OF THEIR STYLE FOR DECADES.

ALTHOUGH THE SHAKERS VIEWED THEMSELVES AS STRICTLY REMOVED FROM THE WORLD, THEY WERE IN many ways unable to escape being a part of their time. Nothing illustrates this no-man-is-an-island truth better than the Believers' clothing. Upon the religion's inception, Shaker dress reflected the working-class styles of the world the Believers were seeking to leave behind—styles that were then adapted in accordance with the simpler Shaker philosophy.

In 1774, when the Shakers left England for America, it was customary for all men to wear knee breeches and buckled shoes. Women, similarly, wore plain dresses. These are the clothes that the early Shakers brought with them when they entered the order of Believers—garments that reflected the agrarian lifestyle of eighteenth-century England and America.

As the Shakers adapted the world's clothing, redefining it in increasingly simple, functional, and modest styles, the resulting garments steadily became more and more archaic. The continuing evolution of Shaker clothing was never based on issues of style, but on pragmatic concerns—what worked best for the wearer and the community at large. It was this clinging to utilitarian fashion (fashion being a misnomer when applied to the Shakers) that increasingly helped to set the Believers apart as oddities in their time.

Although the Shakers had clothing that was distinctive from the fashions of the day, and although they went to great lengths to ensure uniformity among all groups of Believers, the idea that all Shakers looked alike broaches the territory of myth. Despite recurring efforts to achieve a standardized appearance, Shaker communities were simply too far apart for such an attempt to take. Rules for dress issued from central headquarters in New Lebanon were interpreted differently from community to community. Members within a community maintained a homogenous attire, but this uniform might vary from the dress of Believers in another community. The regional availability of materials, as well as an area's climate, no doubt influenced the type of clothing worn by residents of any given community.

Not surprisingly for a celibate faith, guidelines on the appropriateness of male and female dress, and interaction of the sexes in the process of clothing, were strict: "Sisters must not mend, nor set buttons on Brethren's clothes while they have them on." It might have gone without saying, but laws also dictated that "brethren and sisters must not wear each other's clothes, nor be trying them on for any occasion whatever."

▲ BRETHREN

Although there was not absolute homogeny of dress throughout all Shaker communities, a generic uniform did exist. The evolution of the typical Shaker wardrobe started slowly in the early part of the nineteenth century, well after Mother Ann's death. Men's coats and vests became understated and functional, with a small collar and a cape on the jacket. Initially, buttons were removed and replaced with hooks and eyes. As some Shaker communities matured, buttons sometimes reappeared on men's clothing. These were dull steel, however, never a shiny brass.

Shoe buckles characteristic of the time were discarded by the Shakers as nonfunctional and earthly; they were replaced with eyelets and shoelaces.

The full-sleeved white shirt associated today with portraits of patriots was replaced with shirts in dull tones that were more practical for work. These shirts pulled over the head and had cuffless sleeves ending at the elbow, thereby eliminating the need for buttons and making the shirt especially practical for work. With its loose, pleated body, the shirt was comfortable for its wearer even when he was engaged in heavy tasks of lifting, carrying, and bending. This easy garb became a staple in the brethren's work uniform for many years.

Dull knee breeches of blue and brown eventually were replaced with trousers that were more suitable for working and that followed the fashion of the rest of America. Early trousers had a laced up, V-shaped inset that made the waist adjustable and also held them secure. In the nineteenth century, suspenders were used to serve this purpose.

Courtesy: The Winterthur Library: The Edward Deming Andrews Memorial Shaker Collection

■ THIS GROUP OF SHAKER ELDERS IS WEARING THE SIMPLE, DARK CLOTHES AND PLAIN SHIRTS WORN BY ALL NINETEENTH-CENTURY BROTHERS.

© Philip M. Zito

In the summer, trousers were made either of linen or a fabric known to early Americans as linsey-woolsey—a combination of linen and wool, as the name implies. In winter, of course, wool was the material of choice. Butternut-colored pantaloons also were a part of the standard uniform.

Black hats with rounded crowns and broad brims were part of every man's wardrobe, Shaker or worldly, in early America. Hatmaking was not an easy profession, but many converts seemed to possess this skill. As time passed, gray wool, felt, and fur headgear made on wooden forms in community shops replaced the original hat. Though these were made in Shaker workrooms, they did reflect the current trends. Summer called for a lightweight hat. These were made of woven straw or palm and fashioned like the winter models.

Sabbath dress was also important to the Shakers. Brothers wore a long coat usually of a steel-gray color, though this varied with the times. The coat often was removed during the dancing part of the religious service. A vest of the same fabric, cut below a man's natural waistline, gave tidiness to the pious prancing. Drab-colored, then blue, wool trousers completed the lower half of a man's ensemble; these were replaced by cotton or linen in blue or a fine blue stripe in the summer.

Interestingly, the Shakers' desire for uniformity initially resulted in all men's coats being cut the same length, so that while one brother might wear an ankle-length coat, another might be wearing his above the knees. Naturally, in the eyes of the world, this did not make for a group of dapper men.

It wasn't appearances, however, that prompted the Shakers to change. The only thing they appreciated more than uniformity was practicality. Cutting outerwear from a single pattern was simply too dysfunctional to suit Shaker tastes for long. Soon, coats were being made to fit. Even with this and other technical innovations in the design and production of clothing, however, the general appearance of Shaker attire was plain and unstylish.

Grooming, too, was a matter of order. Hair was kept long, but was trimmed neatly in the back and straight across the forehead. Brethren typically wore beards, although, for a few years, these were forbidden. There was so much disgruntlement, however, that the elders soon rescinded the clean-shaven law.

Like other religious communities disassociated with "the world," the Shakers found that their separatism meant that they must internally provide for all their basic needs. Clothing, then, was an early concern for such a fast-growing society. A tailor shop was one of the first operations in the original New Lebanon community, and as Shakerism spread, new families were taught how to open their own shops.

North Wind Picture Archives

■ *OPPOSITE PAGE:* THIS SIMPLE, BROAD BRIM HAT WAS ESSENTIAL TO THE WARDROBE OF EVERY BROTHER, AND WAS MADE IN SHAKER SHOPS. *ABOVE:* SHAKER CLOTHING WOULD SEE LITTLE CHANGE FOR DECADES.

▲ **SISTERS**   Shaker sisters' clothing followed the same basic evolution, starting with the rural dress of the American settler and leading to an increasingly simpler and more utilitarian style. As they were gathered in to their respective communities, sisters brought their personal clothing. But even those humble possessions, following Shaker law, were stripped of any ornamentation, including buttons.

Mother Ann disallowed jewelry as prideful. "You may let the moles and bats have them; that is, the children of this world; for they set their hearts upon such things; but the people of God do not want them." After all, this was a religious sect based on humility.

In the early years, there were basic summer and winter dresses. Summer found sisters in dark blue or black linen dresses styled with elbow-length sleeves and a small, high, collarless neckline. Conforming in cut to the simple empire dresses of Europe and America of the early nineteenth century, a straight skirt fell in small delicate pleats or was gored from the bodice.

Winter wool dresses were similar, with tight elbow-length sleeves and a fitted top. Over the dress, sisters wore a blue-and-white striped knee-length overdress. This was topped with an apron nearly as long as the dress, generally in white or blue-and-white check. A shoulder kerchief or shawl of white lawn or linen folded into a large triangle was worn over the shoulders of all women, thus hiding any trace of a bustline. In or about 1801, a collar was introduced to this layered ensemble, fastening under the scarf that covered the neck. By the first quarter of the nineteenth century, sleeves became long, thus finally covering any trace of skin from the face down.

■ SHAKER SISTERS WEARING DRESSES WITH BERTHAS, USED AFTER THE CIVIL WAR.

Courtesy Shakertown at South Union, Museum Collection

© Philip M. Zito/Dunham Tavern Museum Collection

■ A SISTER'S WINTER WOOL DRESS IS SHOWN HUNG ON THE WALL, AS IT WOULD HAVE IN THE DWELLING HOUSE. NOTE THE BONNET HANGING BESIDE IT.

In the period after the Civil War, a curious object of clothing called a bertha was added to the sisters' wardrobe. The bertha—a half cape or buttoned bib that replaced the neckerchief—was made to match the dress. It was cut in a semicircle pattern, long and low to (nearly touching) the waist. A row of buttons was used to fasten it, thus giving the sisters an updated look to their otherwise old-fashioned appearance. This, as with most Shaker

decisions, was not the only reason for the change. The new bertha was made of a heavier material than the linen scarf and was, therefore, less likely to wrinkle. Made of one flat piece of fabric, it also was easier to construct. Often, the bertha was replete with its own collar, eliminating the need for a separate piece of clothing. By the time this feature was added, the laws governing dress were so relaxed that the bertha was seldom seen without trim such as fringe, rickrack, or, most often, lace.

■ *ABOVE:* THE SHAKER SISTERS' CLOAKS ARE KNOWN FOR THEIR FINE QUALITY AND STYLISH LOOK. THIS ONE IS FROM SOUTH UNION, KENTUCKY. *RIGHT:* THIS IS AN ACTUAL PALM LEAF BONNET, FROM SOUTH UNION, KENTUCKY.

North Wind Picture Archives

SISTERS IN EVERYDAY COSTUME.

■ AT LEFT ARE TWO SISTERS, ONE IN THE UNIVERSAL TIGHT CAP (RIGHT), THE OTHER IN THE UNIQUE PALM LEAF BONNET (LEFT).

Skirts, too, changed in time, becoming much fuller so that they often required ten yards of fabric. They hung to the floor from the natural waist in narrow, unpressed pleats.

Every adult woman wore a tight cap, gathered to conform to the head. Such a cap was given to a sister when she entered the family, and these headdresses are still worn today by the handful of remaining Shaker sisters.

Hair was short for the period, parted in the middle and pulled tight to the back in a bun. Again, practicality with the Shakers overruled style. All farm women of this period wore small, flat headgear called "chip" hats over their caps, and sisters took this fashion into communities with them. Later, they adopted a Quaker bonnet that was more comfortable to wear while working and that was less time-consuming to make. These hats were originally made of paper pasteboard covered in silk.

In 1837, the palm-leaf weaving machine was invented, resulting in the manufacture of a popular woman's bonnet made of palm imported from Cuba. This hat was popular both in the Shaker community and in the outside world. Later, due to political and economic factors, the material was changed from palm to straw, yet the hat remained a fashion staple until the turn of the twentieth century.

■ SHAKER SISTERS FACE THE WORLD FROM THE CHURCH OFFICE AND STORE AT NEW LEBANON, NEW YORK.

Courtesy The Winterthur Library: The Edward Deming Andrews Memorial Shaker Collection

Early Shaker women wore high-heeled shoes (heels of leather-covered wood ranging from 1½ to 2 inches [4 to 5 cm] in height) with buckles, in typical eighteenth-century style. Shaker sisters continued wearing these shoes even long after they were considered obsolete by the rest of the world. Visitors from the outside often commented on how quaint the sisters' footwear was.

This basic work costume, adapted and simplified from the current styles of the world the sisters had left behind, became classic Shaker dress, changing little until church rules were relaxed in this century.

Conformity in grooming and dress was a most important factor in the Shaker community, not only for its practical advantages, but because it also reduced the likelihood of committing the sins of covetousness and envy. In this, as in all other matters of the Shaker life, uniformity reflected Believers' establishment of a heaven on earth. In fact, one Sister had a vision of heaven in which, she reported, all the angels were dressed exactly as Shaker sisters dressed on earth.

This was not the view that many outsiders shared when visiting Shaker communities, however. Although they complimented the sisters on their domestic skills, many visitors thought the pale hooded figures looked extremely unhealthy and unattractive.

One traveler to a Shaker community in the mid-nineteenth century observed that the sisters' dress "is certainly the most ingenious device that was ever contrived for concealing all personal advantages. A bulbous-shaped muslin cap that hides all the hair and covers half the face; a long narrow dress with the waist at the arm-pit, so fashioned that the shoulders all look equally high, the neck covered with a little square white handkerchief, pinned down before, and a pocket handkerchief, folded in a small square, and pinned near the region of the heart, or thrown waiterwise over the arm, constitute a costume that would disguise the very Goddess of Beauty."

Some sisters' Sabbath-day dresses were white, symbolizing the wearers' purity. Older members of the society frequently wore white with a pale blue stripe. As always, the kerchief was fastened about the shoulders, and, for this holy day, an additional large handkerchief was folded over the left arm as a symbol of the woman's willingness to serve. For the worship services, sisters' heads were covered with their caps of starched lawn; these effectively hid the face from any side view.

Sabbath shoes, on the other hand, were often of a bright blue that reminded the sisters of heaven. This, again, led to various worldly opinions on the sisters' appearance—everything from "a crowd of saints" to "a gaggle of geese."

▲ **CHILDREN**   Although the Shakers celebrated their celibacy, they were never without children. Many of the early converts headed large families, and they brought their children with them when they joined the community of Believers. In addition, from the beginning of their communal lifestyle, the Shakers accepted foundlings and unwanted children into their communities, giving them love and an education in the hope that when they came of age, they would join the church.

These youngsters were generally dressed as miniature adults, their clothing distinguishable only by fabric and color, not cut.

Little girls wore long dresses and neckerchiefs like the mature women. They were allowed to go bareheaded until the age of ten. At this time they began to cover their heads demurely with nets. As they reached puberty, or by about age fourteen, they started wearing bonnets. At this time, they were considered women, not girls, and took on the work and the responsibilities of an adult.

Fabric for young girls' dresses featured a little more color than that which comprised a sister's wardrobe, and some pattern was permitted. Let there be no mistake, though—Shaker girls were not allowed to be too festive or gay; they were required to follow many of the rules governing Shaker life.

Male children dwelling in the Shaker communities wore trousers and the distinctive pullover, loosefitting smock or shirt worn by all adult men. On formal occasions—Sundays and holidays—Shaker boys wore vest coats varying only in fabric and color from those worn by the brethren.

Overall, these male children looked like diminutive versions of the adults in their communities, because of the shape and cut of their garments. As with Shaker girls, though, boys were given clothing made of a different fabric content than that of the men's. For example, men's vests generally were made of a cotton and wool blend, while a boy's vest would be all cotton. Never capricious, the utilitarian Shakers must have had reasons for making such distinctions: Cotton was less costly for a growing boy, for one thing. And as for girls being allowed printed or more colorful materials for their dresses, it should be remembered that a printed fabric, and colors, shows less soil than a light solid, thus reducing the laundering labors of Shaker women.

The distinction between children's and adult's clothing intimated an even greater separation of the two groups in community life: Shaker children did not reside in dwelling houses with adults, but in separate living quarters—boys living in one house, girls in another, with each house governed by an elder.

Courtesy The Winterthur Library: The Edward Deming Andrews Memorial Shaker Collection

■ CHILDREN AND ADULTS, POSED ON WHEELBARROWS, AT THE WATERVLIET, NEW YORK, SHAKER COMMUNITY, ARE DRESSED VIRTUALLY IDENTICALLY.

▲ TEXTILES FOR THE OUTSIDE WORLD

Because of their separation from the rest of the world, Shaker societies, by necessity, had to become self-sufficient. The production of fabric and clothing in Shaker shops was a direct result of having to provide internally the clothing for all the members of the community. And because each task in a community was thought of as a type of meditation, there was a constant refining of technique and quality in the manufacture of fabric and clothing.

Eventually, as the workshops became more and more efficient, there was surplus production. Never wasteful, the Shakers promptly made these goods available for outside sale. Before any commerce was engaged in, however, the needs of the society always were met first—needs not only of the family producing the goods, but also the needs of less fortunate or newly-formed communities.

▲ CLOTHING

Clothing that was sold to the world included fine Shaker-knitted baby articles such as booties, sweaters, and shawl and cap sets. These were of such outstanding quality that the best department stores clamored to stock them.

Several Shaker families made a profitable business of selling exceptionally made cloaks from around 1890 to the outbreak of the Second World War. A colorful cloak called the ''Dorothy'' cloak, after its designer, Elder Dorothy Ann Durgin of Canterbury, New Hampshire, was extremely popular—so much so that President Grover Cleveland's wife ordered one to wear to her husband's presidential inauguration in 1893. The sisters who filled Mrs. Cleveland's order took such pride in their work that they insisted on making her a second cloak, holding that the first one was in some way flawed.

That first flawed cloak still exists, and the alleged blemish is so imperceptible that no one has been able to find it.

▲ OTHER TEXTILES

Most of the textiles sold to non-Believers were household, rather than personal, items—rugs, bed and table linens, towels, cushions, chair tapes, and blankets. This does not mean, however, that these textiles were produced solely for outside sale: All items made in Shaker textiles shops were things potentially needed and used by the community itself. Shaker thinking held that the world was sinful enough without sisters and brothers adding to its guilt with a glut of superfluous material goods.

Chairs are perhaps the most famous of Shaker products. By the Civil War, these chairs were enormously popular all over the country. Rush and splint seats, which had been used for years, were replaced with new and comfortable taped seats.

© Richard Day/Shakertown at South Union, KY

■ *OPPOSITE PAGE: IN ITS SPARE, INDUSTRIAL SIMPLICITY, A SEWING ROOM AT SOUTH UNION, KENTUCKY, HAS ITS OWN SORT OF BEAUTY. ABOVE: THIS SHAKER SEWING TABLE IS EFFICIENT AND ATTRACTIVE, AWAITING THE HANDS OF A SISTER.*

© Kenneth Martin/Armstock/Hancock Shaker Village, MA

■ THIS ELEGANTLY SIMPLE ROOM SETTING AT THE HANCOCK SHAKER VILLAGE FEATURES A FINE BRAIDED RAG RUG AND A SIMPLE, ALMOST CONTEMPORARY LOOKING WOOD STOVE.

Handwoven tapes were mostly wool, but some were made of linen and cotton. Twenty to thirty yards (18 to 27 m) of tape were required to construct just one chair seat, so communities had to produce literally thousands of yards of tape to keep up with the demand.

Later, most of the tape was purchased from manufacturers outside the community and woven by sisters into the chairs.

This special woven seat was the forerunner of today's modern webbed lawn chair. It featured interesting patterns and arrangements of contrasting colors, thus explaining much of its popularity. (Instructions for taping a chair are found on page 72.)

Shaker workshops were noted for their particularly fine and attractive rag carpets, sewn together in strips to make large area rugs or runners. These had a functional origin in providing warmth and reducing noise in a community's large dwelling houses. Needless to say, these rag rugs also added a bit of pattern and color to the otherwise stark interiors.

Runners measuring up to eighty feet (24 m) long were made for hallways in dwellings. In buildings with scrubbed and polished bare wood floors that were walked upon daily by a hundred people or more, the noise reduction alone offered by these rugs would have merited their use. In addition, they spared at least some wear on the floors.

Shakers created direction and rhythm in their rugs by twisting together rags of different colors in the warp, during the weaving process. This made it easy to produce diagonal stripes and twists in the rug's pattern. Most often, a rug featured an overall design, which repeated itself in cheerful colors.

To complete a rug visually and to make it sturdy, the Shakers finished it with bindings or borders on two or all four sides. When rugs were stitched together to make a large carpet, it was extremely important to the Shakers that all adjoining pieces were carefully matched.

Rugs were bejeweled in rich colors: green, black, brown, rose, purple, and gold, as well as the favorite combination of red and blue. For Shakers surrounded with walls of white, these rugs were something of a diversion—a surprising jolt of color in an otherwise monochromatic lifestyle.

Hundreds of blankets were needed to maintain the Shaker community's needs. Some were bought ready-made, and others were simply plain wool cut straight off the bolt. Colors were usually gray, blue, or white. But even in this mundane area, there were governing laws: "Only two colors are to be used on bed coverings." In practice, though, often a third or fourth color found its way into the blanket. Blue and white seems to have been the preferred color scheme.

The design of Shaker blankets stems from function—from the way the blanket was made on looms—rather than from conscious aesthetics. Geometric patterns (a grid or tattersall plaid) were never embellished with any other design or embroidery, as were similar blankets made by outside mills that catered to the Victorian taste. Blankets were hemmed on the sides and never displayed fringe ornamentation.

Shakers also made coverlets and quilts, extra bedcovers that apparently were regarded as a necessity in coping with bitter New England winters. Coverlets were more elaborate than blankets, displaying rich colorful plaids with evenly-spaced tufts of contrasting yarn. These yarn tufts secured the coverlets to a solid flannel liner.

© Jeanetta Ho/Dunham Tavern Museum Collection

■ THESE HANDSOME SHAKER BEDCOVERS ARE ON DISPLAY AT THE
DUNHAM TAVERN MUSEUM. SIMPLE AND FUNCTIONAL, THESE
BEDCOVERS WERE OF SUPERB QUALITY AND DESIGN.

Shaker quilts were unremarkable, from a design standpoint, for their day (unlike the flamboyant Amish quilts of the same period). However, Shaker quilts are noted for their fine needlework. In addition to excellence in stitching, a few surviving Shaker crazy quilts from the turn of the nineteenth century also exhibit an unusually decorative flair. These quilts only appeared, however, well after Shaker laws had become relaxed.

All in all, Shaker bedcovers and blankets, through their simplicity and functionalism, reached a high level of excellence for household items otherwise considered ordinary. Theirs is a subtle beauty, attained through simplicity of manufacture and design, as well as through astute use of limited color.

▲ ENTRY INTO COMMERCE

The Shakers' entry into commerce began with goods first being sold to outsiders visiting the Shaker shops. Soon, Shaker wares found their way to merchants in neighboring communities.

By the late nineteenth century, pincushions in the shape of strawberries, Shaker-made doll clothes, and a wide selection of household fancywork items joined the more utilitarian goods first produced and sold by Shaker women. These handmade products were eagerly purchased by tourists as souvenirs from the on-site stores operated by each Shaker society.

▲ WEAVING SHOPS

The production of textiles in the Shaker weaving shops, both for the community itself and for the outside world, is one of the most fascinating aspects of Shaker enterprise. The Shakers' drive for economic independence and unsurpassed quality incited great innovation.

Upon the inception of the Shaker communities in the eighteenth century, linen and wool were the primary fibers available to Believers residing in New England. Flax, from which linen is spun, was grown universally into the mid-nineteenth century. Sisters processed the flax into fibers for linen thread, and, careful to allow nothing to go to waste, turned over the seeds of the flax plants for processing into linseed oil.

Shakers began using cotton when the invention of the cotton gin in 1793 simplified processing of the fiber in America. For years, sisters spun and manufactured their own cotton

■ THIS PATENTED OHIO RUG LOOM AT SOUTH UNION, KENTUCKY, IS TYPICAL OF THE LOOMS USED BY SHAKER COMMUNITIES AS THEY MOVED INTO THE COMMERCIAL MAINSTREAM.

© Richard Day/Shakertown at South Union, KY

© Jeanetta Ho/Dunham Tavern Museum Collection

■ THIS SHAKER YARN WINDER WAS USED IN PROCESSING HIGH-QUALITY WOOLEN YARN FOR THE SHAKER'S OWN USE, AS WELL AS FOR PRODUCTS MADE FOR COMMERCIAL MARKETS.

threads and fabrics from raw cotton purchased from southern vendors. (The communities in Kentucky, however, even grew their own cotton, having a suitable climate. They, too, though, eventually ended up buying, rather than raising, their cotton.)

By the 1860s, high-quality cotton and linen threads were available for the Shakers to purchase at reasonable prices to fashion into clothing. Even though purchasing materials from outside the community curtailed the Shakers' total self-sufficiency a bit, being sensible, Believers recognized the time and dollar savings this would afford. Gradually, Shaker sisters gave up the time-consuming practice of hand-processing their own cotton and linen fibers.

Starting out, all Shaker communities raised their own sheep for both wool and food. The New Lebanon society, for instance, was known for its fine flocks of Merino and Saxon sheep. But as communities matured and civilization became more reliant on technology, wool, too, became a costly enterprise for most communities to process into yarn and cloth. Sisters eventually nodded to modernity, purchasing commercially produced wool yarns. But although they forfeited some of their self-sufficiency for convenience, the Shakers refused to sacrifice quality. The same high standards that went into production of their own fibers were applied to their selection of commercial goods. Shakers only traded with the best suppliers, even going so far as to purchase extremely costly European wools on a routine basis for their exquisite capes and coats.

The production of silk in the Shaker communities is a remarkable, little-known aspect of the Shaker textiles industry. The relatively warm climates of the Ohio and Kentucky communities were most favorable to silkworm production, although almost all Shaker communities attempted to raise silkworms.

A great deal of work was necessary to make silk. Mulberry trees had to be grown for their leaves, which served as food for the worms. Shaker children gathered the leaves and helped the sisters work the cocoons to spin into thread.

Silk production reached its crest at North Union, Kentucky, at about the time of the Civil War. But even then, only a small amount of silk was available to sell to the outside world. After the war, production dropped sharply.

But during the peak days, the fiber was not an uncommon sight within a community, especially during formal events. Shaker sisters and brothers both sported fine silk kerchiefs and ties for special occasions. The majority of silk was used for small clothing accessories, rather than as full dresses or shirts. Because of the time and tedious work involved in raising the worms, processing the thread, and handweaving the fabric, it is obvious that the Shakers had a great appreciation for the presence of silk in their wardrobes.

Silk also afforded one of the few opportunities for sisters to wear bright colors like magenta. By changing the color of warp and weft threads, sisters were able to create an iridescent effect that was not available in other types of fabric.

The Shakers also experimented with some unusual fibers, with varying success. One of their more absorbing ventures was in the production of palm-leaf fiber for fans, table mats, and hats.

Special equipment was invented by the Shakers for weaving a palm-leaf material, and Believers imported palm leaves from Cuba to supply their needs. The result was a beautiful, tightly woven material that enjoyed a high level of popularity, especially when fashioned into women's bonnets that were sold to the outside world.

After the Civil War, it became difficult to import palm leaves and rye and oat straw produced on the community farm was substituted.

On a small scale, the Shakers experimented with local game animals such as raccoons, opossums, rabbits, and beavers, and sometimes even cats, for making yarn or felted fabrics. Knitted gloves were often a product of these fabrics. Shakers were never unkind to animals. Even when using them for food, they found the most humane way of dispatching them.

Another Shaker innovation was poplar cloth. Around 1860 Shakers developed a process for turning wood from the poplar tree into a fine cloth with a texture much like paper. Poplar cloth was not used for clothing, however, but to cover boxes. Because the poplar tree is useless as furniture wood or firewood, the Shakers were demonstrating an efficient utilization of a readily available, inexpensive New England resource. Shaker poplar cloth was regarded as an attractive and stylish material all over the world.

© Jeanetta Ho/Dunham Tavern Museum Collection

■ *LEFT:* FLAX, FOR LINEN, WAS A UNIVERSAL PRODUCT IN EARLY NINETEENTH-CENTURY AMERICA. THESE SHAKER FLAX COMBERS WERE USED IN THE PRODUCTION OF LINEN. *FOLLOWING PAGE:* AN EVOCATIVE VIEW INTO A NEARLY VANISHED, PASTORAL WORLD. THE SHEEP AND SHAKER FENCE ARE AT PLEASANT HILL, KENTUCKY.

© Richard Day/Shakertown at South Union, KY

Chapter Four

▲▲▲

INDUSTRIES

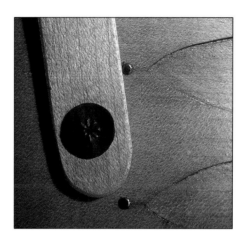

"Trifles make perfection, but perfection
is no trifle."

SHAKER SAYING

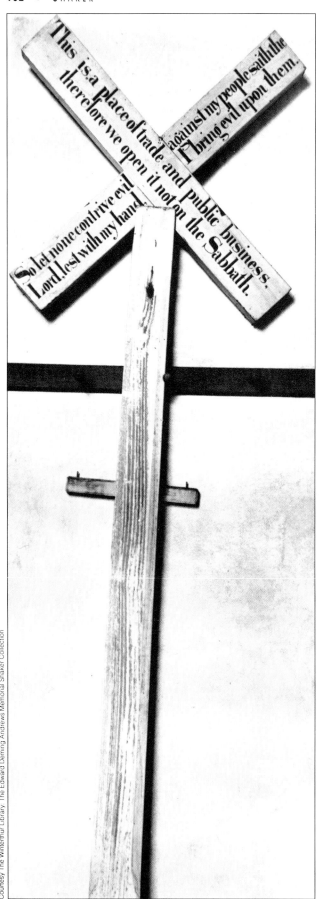

Courtesy The Winterthur Library: The Edward Deming Andrews Memorial Shaker Collection

WHEN APPLIED TO THE SHAKERS, THE TERM "CRAFT" REALLY IS A MISNOMER. NOTHING COULD SMACK less of a hobby or a very pleasant but unessential pastime than the Believers' approach to handmade products. A more correct description for the products they created is industry, for, indeed, every one of the Shakers' handmade goods was its own industry and was treated as such.

In each endeavor, however small, the Shakers had a precise and well-defined purpose. Apostate David Lawson, who left the community in 1845, succinctly captured the Shaker philosophy: "This people [sic] are strict utilitarians. In all they do, the first inquiry is, 'Will it be useful?'"

No industry was entered into by the Shakers unless it answered a real need. Goods were sold to the outside world only after the Shakers' own needs within the community were met, and even then, only those items the Shakers themselves could use were made for the external market. But the Shakers made no apologies for entering into commerce. Although they were separatists on many levels, Believers were realists and pragmatists in matters of finance; they never attempted to sever economic ties with the world, but recognized the need for open trade.

To be accurate, furniture should top the list in any discussion of Shaker industries, for it was easily the most important. Yet because of its significance and the extent of its production, furniture more conveniently is considered as a category unto itself. The other Shaker industries—oval wooden boxes, woven baskets, iron stoves, flat brooms, an assortment of sewing and kitchen accessories, and more—share with furniture several characteristic design principles.

All Shaker industries anticipated the Bauhaus design philosophy of the early twentieth century, a philosophy often articulated by the Shakers themselves, including such tenets as form following function, the use of natural, indigenous materials and simple, clean lines. As early as 1824, a full century before the advent of the international school of modern architecture, Shakers were saying, "that is best which works best." Whether basket or stove, Shaker products featured an advanced degree of functionalism, with minimal extraneous parts or embellishment—all in all, a high-minded aesthetic.

This purist aesthetic translates, in virtually every Shaker industry, as beauty. One of the last surviving Shakers, Elder Bertha Lindsay of Canterbury, New Hampshire, eloquently capsulized the Shaker view in a brochure, *Industries and Inventions of the Shakers*: "Some have asked—why did the Shakers invent so much—why did such beauty abound in their work—I can only say—The beauty of the world about us is only according to what we ourselves bring to it. For example: To some, Autumn is a prelude to winter with its cold and loneliness. To others, Autumn represents the magnificence of God's Great Creations . . . . With you and only you, lies the choice . . . . I like the words of the poet, who, looking on the beauty of Autumn, said, 'Dear Lord, when with this life I'm thru and I make my abode with you, Just one thing I would ask of thee. Will Heaven have Autumn, and crimson tree?''

© Jeff Greenberg/Hancock Shaker Village, MA

■ *OPPOSITE PAGE:* A PRAGMATIC PEOPLE, THE SHAKERS RECOGNIZED THE NEED FOR COMMERCE, BUT THEY PRIORITIZED IT WELL BEHIND THEIR HIGHEST MISSION: TO WORSHIP AND SERVE GOD. *LEFT:* AMONG ALL SHAKER INDUSTRIES, FURNITURE MAKING WAS MOST PROLIFIC AND PROFITABLE.

▲ OVAL BOXES

Next to furnishings, the best-known Shaker industry is wooden oval boxes. These are known to have been produced at New Lebanon as early as 1798, and by the close of the nineteenth century, oval boxes were available in nearly every Shaker community. The last Shaker brother, Delmer Wilson, died at the Sabbathday Lake, Maine, community in 1961; until then, he kept up the oval-box industry by himself, if only on a small scale.

Oval boxes usually were sold in nests of graduated sizes, the earliest consisting of twelve boxes, then nine, and the later ones of seven and five. It was not until 1833 that they were referred to as oval boxes; until then, they were called "nests" of boxes.

Boxes were made in any number of sizes to accommodate a variety of uses in the households and workshops. They were used to hold everything except water. By 1834, boxes were numbered according to size. The largest—numbers one, two, three, four, and five—were the best sellers.

The tops of the boxes were usually made of pine, while the bentwood rims, which were precisely joined with slender "fingers" that are the boxes' most distinctive trait, typically were made of maple. Finished boxes were either painted or varnished.

The graceful fingers, called "swallowtails" by the Shakers, were held in place by small copper tacks that wouldn't rust and ruin the wood. Tacks were meticulously aligned—one more example of the Shakers' ongoing attention to detail and attempt at perfection.

■ *RIGHT:* BOXES IN GRADUATED SIZES WERE PRODUCED IN BRETHREN'S WORKSHOPS IN HANCOCK, MASSACHUSETTS, AS WELL AS IN MOST OTHER SHAKER COMMUNITIES. *OPPOSITE PAGE:* THE SLENDER FINGERS THAT ALLOW WOOD TO EXPAND ARE AN IMPORTANT TRAIT OF SHAKER OVAL BOXES, AS IS PERFECT ALIGNMENT OF THE TACKS.

© Kenneth Martin/Amstock/Hancock Shaker Village, MA

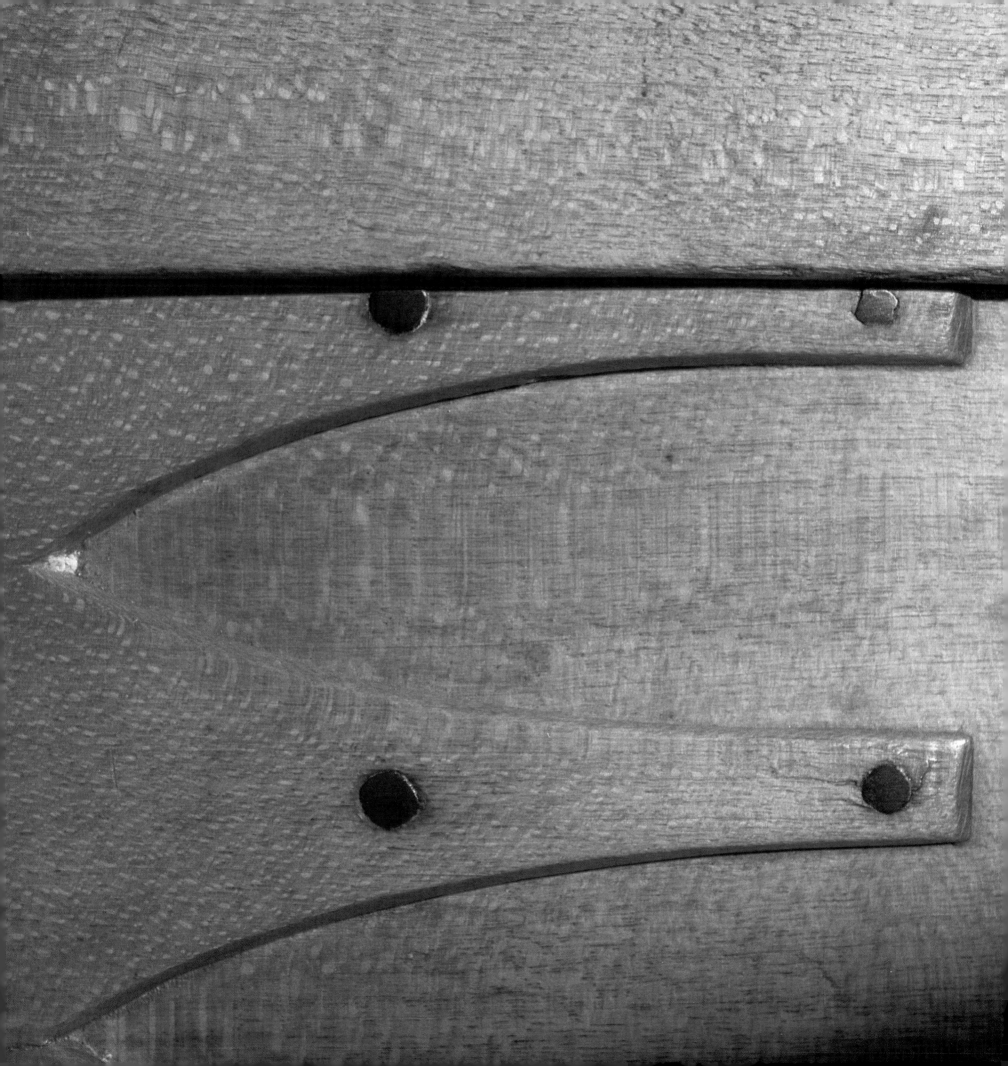

© Philip M. Zito/Golden Lamb, OH

■ *ABOVE:* WOODEN BOXES IN GRADUATED SIZES SERVED ANY NUMBER OF UTILITARIAN FUNCTIONS. *RIGHT:* MADE PRODUCTION-STYLE VERSUS ONE PIECE AT A TIME, OVAL BOXES WERE CONSTRUCTED IN PARTS, AS SEEN BY THIS PHOTOGRAPH IN THE BRETHREN'S WORKSHOP IN HANCOCK SHAKER VILLAGE.

While the Shakers did not invent the finger joints, they did refine and popularize the design. The space between fingers was more than aesthetically pleasing: It was growing room that allowed the maple sides to expand and contract without buckling, in accordance with changes in humidity and temperature.

If the last Shaker brother, Elder Delmer Wilson, is any indication, brethren were not simply oval-box makers by trade. Instead, they were more like Renaissance men. At various points in his life, Elder Delmer worked at Sabbathday Lake not only as a woodworker but also as a beekeeper, barber, builder, dentist, artist, photographer, and orchardist.

Elder Delmer's jack-of-all-trades lifestyle was a matter of following precedent. Brother Henry Blint was indentured at Canterbury in 1838 at the age of fourteen, at which time he began working in wood. But he also worked on the farm, then in a blacksmith shop. He learned the stove, tinware, and cut nail industries, and at age nineteen, was an instructor of children. He taught his students whiplash braiding, studied printing and binding on the side, moonlighted as a night watchman, and, in season, a harvester. Eventually he became an elder and member of the ministry, occupations that in no way interfered with his practice of dentistry or his vocation as beekeeper.

As exquisite and demanding of specialized skills as they appear, oval boxes weren't by any means an all-consuming industry; they were only one of many trades practiced by any one Shaker brother.

© Kenneth Martin/Armstock/Hancock Shaker Village, MA

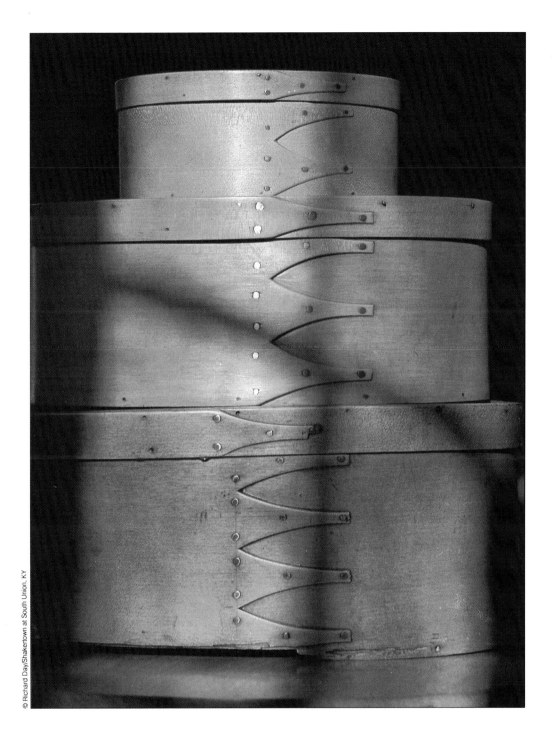

© Richard Day/Shakertown at South Union, KY

■ DESPITE THEIR UTILITARIANISM, BEAUTIFULLY FINGERED OVAL SHAKER WOODEN BOXES ARE INHERENTLY AESTHETIC IN THEIR METICULOUS WORKMANSHIP AND UNSUPERFLUOUS DESIGN. PICTURED HERE ARE BOXES FROM SOUTH UNION, KENTUCKY.

An 1890 issue of *The Manifesto* recorded the improved methods of production that were happily adopted by Shakers: "At first the rims were cut from the log in a common saw mill . . . . In 1830 a buzz saw did the work of cutting out the rims." In 1822, the rims and tops, until then planed by hand, were planed by machine. The fingers themselves eventually were machine-cut. Although the components were made using a machine, there was nothing automated or impersonal about the process. Individual attention was required in each step, the machine serving as little more than a more precise and efficient extension of the hand.

Courtesy The Winterthur Library: The Edward Deming Andrews Memorial Shaker Collection

■ *ABOVE:* THE PLETHORA OF BUILT-IN CUPBOARDS THAT GRACED EVERY SHAKER BUILDING REQUIRED AN OUTPOURING OF BURNED WOODEN KNOBS AND SCREWS FROM THE BRETHREN'S WORKSHOPS. *RIGHT:* WOODENWARE CRAFTED BY BRETHREN WAS DIVERSE, INCLUDING PAILS, CARRIERS, BUCKETS, AND OTHER ITEMS.

▲ OTHER WOODENWARE

More than oval boxes were produced in Shaker woodshops. A closely related item was the Shaker oval carrier. Like the box, it featured copper-tacked fingers for the expansion of wood. It was made in all of the eastern communities from the beginning of the nineteenth century, and it continued to be produced at Sabbathday Lake until 1960.

Another popular item that was made until midway through this century was the cheese hoop. Production began early on, too, probably not long after the first communities gathered. The hoops were used in the cheese-making process to press the curds. Lined with cheesecloth and filled with curds, the hoop was placed in a press, which was screwed down by degrees until the cheese was hard.

Other products of the woodenware industry—dry measures, scoops, mortars and pestles, buckets, pails, tubs, kegs, bowls, and shovels—also met the everyday needs of the cook. Dry measures were made of hard wood such as ash, and were made both with and without handles and lids.

Wooden scoops or dippers, most often of ash or maple, also were made soon after the first Shaker communities formed. The first recorded sale of scoops was in 1789. Like oval boxes, dippers frequently were sold in nests; usually there were three to a nest.

The production of wooden pails, tubs, barrels, and casks known as coopers' ware began shortly after Believers gathered in the first village at New Lebanon. Records from 1789 show several entries of "sundry coopers' ware." Thereafter, entries became more specific,

© Philip M. Zito/Dunham Tavern Museum Collection

Courtesy The Winterthur Library: The Edward Deming Andrews Memorial Shaker Collection

© Richard Day/Shakertown at South Union, KY

■ *ABOVE, LEFT:* AS SELF-SUFFICIENT UTOPIAS, EACH SHAKER COMMUNITY INCLUDED ENTERPRISES NECESSARY FOR DAILY LIFE, SUCH AS THE COBBLER'S SHOP AT NEW LEBANON, NEW YORK. *ABOVE, RIGHT:* AN AGRICULTURAL ECONOMY DICTATED THE PRODUCTION OF ESSENTIAL TOOLS SUCH AS THIS WOODEN GRAIN SHOVEL AND HAYFORK FROM SOUTH UNION, KENTUCKY.

naming individual items such as tubs or churns. Coopers' ware was a solid industry for only about twenty-five years, however. Lack of lumber was cited as a primary reason for the wane. A small amount of coopers' ware continued to be produced until the close of the nineteenth century, however, to supply the community's internal needs for containers such as apple barrels, butter and lard firkins, seed pails, churns, and wash and dye tubs. Like other Shaker wares, tubs and pails were made in various sizes and were sold in nests of threes. Early pails featured "wood-loops," which later were replaced, for a slightly higher price, with band-iron.

© Kenneth Martin/Amstock/Hancock Shaker Village, MA

■ HANDWOVEN BASKETS UNDOUBTEDLY ARE ONE OF THE MOST BELOVED LEGACIES OF THE SHAKER SISTERS. SHOWN HERE IS AN ARRAY FROM HANCOCK, MASSACHUSETTS.

▲ **BASKETS** A close contender for the title of article most recognizably Shaker is the woven wooden basket. Made in multitudinous patterns to suit many uses, the Shaker basket is appreciated today, as it was in the past, for its intricacy of construction and delicacy of appearance.

The first baskets of woven white poplar were made by Shaker sisters in 1813. Because all Shaker work was approached as industry, rather than craft, systems were devised to streamline production.

In their cabinetshops, brethren carved the wooden forms upon which the baskets were to be woven. Basket handles and rims were also made by brethren in their shops. The wooden forms used for weaving corresponded to similar molds used in making the handles and rims, so that a near-perfect fit was guaranteed, with nothing left to chance. In contrast, other woven baskets of the day typically were a one-person effort; less systematic than the Shaker approach, these efforts, by comparison, appeared crude and haphazard.

For several years, Shaker sisters annually issued a new design to their offerings of small poplar baskets. The styles included cap baskets, both with and without lids, as well as cat head, kitten head, knife, spoon, sugar bowl, fancy, card, demijohn, box, and hexagon box baskets, among others.

Poplar was used exclusively on the small fancy baskets. Shaker sisters also wove larger baskets from split black ash for the heavier household and farm chores. As with everything Shaker, need determined production, and function determined form. "Conscience baskets," for example, were made large and shallow for use in the laundry houses and weaving shops. Egg baskets required a smaller scale, tighter weave, and greater depth—in effect, simulating a snug and sturdy nest.

Fruit baskets were made in special sizes and designs to accommodate the harvesting of specific fruits. Thus, there were cherry baskets, grape baskets, plum baskets, and others. Among the most capacious baskets were those for storing roots and herbs. Chip baskets featured a special protective leather lining for the collection of fire kindling and wood chips.

Records from the New Lebanon basket shop in 1837 reveal that at least seventy-six different types of baskets were produced that year, including everything from a three-inch (7.5 cm) poplar sewing basket to a six-foot (1.8-m) split black ash basket for roots, herbs, and bark.

While the Shakers were great inventors, invention for its own sake never was their goal. Innovations occurred with inordinate frequency among Shakers because of their desire for efficiency. The less time spent completing a chore, the more time for worship—the Shakers' highest priority. When an existing means of operation already offered maximum efficiency, the Shakers saw no need for modification. Basketmaking, according to some early documents, was a case in point. Shakers learned this craft from the masters—neighboring Native Americans—and made few changes in the weaving technique.

Today Shaker basketmaking is undergoing a revival, thanks largely to the efforts of one person, Martha Wetherbee. Her books and classes taught across the country have generated a burgeoning interest in this old craft.

■ THE WOODEN FRAMES UPON WHICH BASKETS WERE WOVEN, AS WELL AS THE HANDLES AND RIMS, WERE MADE BY BRETHREN, WITH SISTERS EXECUTING THE ACTUAL WEAVING.

■ CAST-IRON STOVES WERE MADE AT SHAKER COMMUNITIES ALMOST AS SOON AS BELIEVERS ORGANIZED INTO VILLAGES. NO FIREPLACES, BUT ONLY STOVES, PROVIDED HEAT WITHIN ALL SHAKER BUILDINGS. THESE SHAKER-MADE STOVES ARE ONE-OF-A-KIND IN DESIGN.

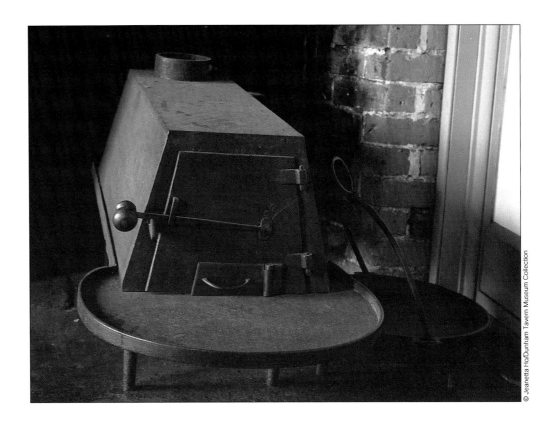

© Jeanetta Ho/Dunham Tavern Museum Collection

▲ **STOVES**   One industry, in particular, exemplifies the functionalism and simplicity of the Shaker design idiom: stoves. In all Shaker buildings, fireplaces housed Shaker-made stoves instead of open fires. In 1795, just two years after the meetinghouse at Shirley, Massachusetts, was constructed, a visitor commented on the stoves—an observation that points to the conclusion that stoves must have been produced in the community soon after the Believers gathered. Foundries at Shirley, as well as at New Lebanon, Hancock, and Harvard were producing a large number of stoves by the early 1800s.

The fundamental design was a simple box, obviously related to the earlier six-plate stove. Each Shaker stove, however, was modified or detailed: Of two hundred stoves documented by a researcher, few are identical. Size and shape vary; some feature legs that are straight, while others are cabriole; some use cast iron and others wrought iron. On all, however, there is the unmistakable stamp of Shaker simplicity. All further share the unusual characteristic of doors that open from left to right.

▲ **TINWARE**   The individual Shaker communities tended to be known for one industry more than another. New Lebanon was recognized for its chairs; Hancock, for its tin.

Tinsmithing was an important industry in all communities, but especially in Hancock. The industry thrived there until the mid-1800s, with wares sold throughout New England.

Like other Shaker industries, tinsmithing began as an answer to the Shakers' own domestic needs. Any number of household items including pitchers, shaving cups, watering pots, funnels, match safes, needle cases, boxes, pans, dust pans, bread and cake tins, sconces, scoops, dippers, and apple corers were made in the tin shops. Only after the community's internal needs were met did the commercial tin trade commence.

▲ OTHER METALWARE

Next to farming, the most important job at a Shaker community was that of the blacksmith. It was in the blacksmith's shop that the tools and nails used in every building project were made. Shovels, axes, saws, scythes, ox-yokes, frying pans, plow-irons, and even iron and steel candlesticks, plus any number of additional items including, of course, horseshoes, were made here.

The surplus was sold—hoes, as early as 1789; cut and wrought nails, as early as 1790. The April 1890 issue of *The Manifesto* recorded that cut and wrought nails were "for several years . . . a source of considerable income. These wrought nails were used in the coarser work while building, until the year 1812 when they were superseded by the cut nails. Wrought nails were also used as early as 1780 for shingling and lathing, but with the introduction of cut nails, soon after the organization of the Community, the wrought nails passed out of use. The machinery for cut nails and the work of forming the heads by a hard hammer, employed not less than twelve persons and yielded a very profitable income." The manufacture of cut nails—which, are believed to have first been used by Shakers—ended in 1830.

■ *Left:* The blacksmith's shop was extremely important to the Shaker community as a source not only of farm implements, but of everything from sad irons to candlesticks. *Above:* Hancock, Massachusetts, was best known for its tinware, a thriving industry till the mid-1800s. Wares included tea sets, as shown, and everything from shaving cups to apple corers.

■ SHAKERS BEGAN RAISING BROOM CORN TO MANUFACTURE THEIR OWN BROOMS AS EARLY AS 1789. INITIALLY, THE BROOMS WERE ROUND, BUT A SHAKER BROTHER IS CREDITED WITH INVENTING THE MORE EFFICIENT FLAT BOTTOM, WHICH SOON MADE THE ROUNDED BROOM OBSOLETE.

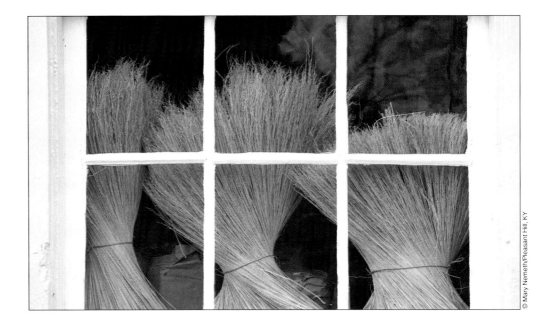

▲ BROOMS

Given the Shaker penchant for cleanliness, it is no surprise that the production of brooms was a significant industry in Shaker communities. Instead of serving as a symbol of drudgery and the mundane, the broom was regarded by Shakers as a respected tool. Rather than being closeted away behind closed doors, the Shaker broom was hung in plain view on the wall.

The first Shakers to raise broom corn and manufacture brooms were those at Watervliet, beginning in 1798. Watervliet brother Theodore Bates is credited with having invented the flat broom, which swept a wider swath than the earlier round broom, which soon became almost obsolete.

It wasn't long before a thriving broom industry was operating at New Lebanon, too. The industry started there no later than 1805 and continued strong throughout the century.

Improvements were made in production as the industry progressed. Initially, the corn was tied onto the turned soft maple broom handle by nothing more than a wheel and shaft, with the broom twine wound about the shaft. A more sophisticated apparatus was invented and used, increasing production to about two dozen brooms per day.

▲ POPLARWARE

Until the Shakers began their poplarware industry, no one had put wood from the poplar tree to good use. Poplar had been regarded as a secondary or junk wood until Believers devised a method of weaving strips of it into jewelry and bureau boxes. These popular boxes became strong sellers in their day and are favorites among today's collectors, as well.

The Shakers split poplar into two-foot-long (60-cm) pieces, which they then froze and planed. The planed strip or shaving was straightened and dried and run through a bank of knives that cut the wood into strips only 1/16 of an inch (1.5 mm) wide. These narrow strips were woven with cotton on a twenty-two-inch-wide (56-cm) loom to produce a woven-wood material not unlike that of the window blinds of recent years. Each Shaker community had a different woven pattern. After the poplar was woven, the fabric was rolled into bolts, then stretched out across work tables where it was cut into shapes and folded into boxes.

Cotton gauze was glued onto the back of the fabric to prevent frazzling. Cotton stuffing was placed over this bandagelike material and was then covered with shiny satin. This soft, filled satin lined the inside of the box. Boxes typically featured white kid leather at the seams and ribbon and buttons as clasps. Production of this unusual craft continued until the 1950s at most communities.

▲ SEWING ACCESSORIES

As important as the sewing industry was for the Shaker sisters, a sewing accessories industry also became significant.

The accessory industry really was a subgroup of the tanning industry. Sewing rolls that unfolded to reveal a seamstress' tools—scissors, thimbles, needles, and more—were made of beautiful glove-soft, incandescent leather. Leather boxes made in various sizes also served as repositories for sewing paraphernalia.

▲ OTHER INDUSTRIES

Braided whiplashes and horsewhips constituted another early industry. Started at New Lebanon, the industry lasted some forty years there, at which time the Watervliet settlement took over the business. Even though the weaving of chair tapes and baskets was conducted by sisters, it was the brethren who braided the tanned horsehides into lashes—perhaps, it may be speculated, because the aggressive utility of the product more closely fit the traditional male stereotype.

At least one Shaker industry, the production of tobacco pipes, reflects historical changes not only in Shaker communities but in America, as a whole. When the Shakers launched their pipe business in New Lebanon, where natural deposits of red clay provided ready material for pipe bowls and stems, smoking was socially acceptable even among Believers. The Millennial Laws, which forbade any number of seemingly innocent actions, censured pipe smoking only in terms of how pipes should be handled to avoid fires. The pipe industry continued until as late as 1853, and it was only after the Civil War that smoking was frowned upon by the Shakers.

■ SEWING ACCESSORIES PRODUCED BY BELIEVERS FOR SALE OUTSIDE THE COMMUNITIES INCLUDED STRAWBERRY-DESIGN PIN CUSHIONS, SEWING BASKETS, AND SEWING ROLLS OF GLOVE-SOFT LEATHER.

© Philip M. Zito/Dunham Tavern Museum Collection

© Kenneth Martin/Amstock/Hancock Shaker Village, MA

Chapter Five

▲▲▲

FEEDING A
COMMUNITY

"Shaker your plate" [waste not]

BROTHER DELMER WILSON, SABBATHDAY LAKE

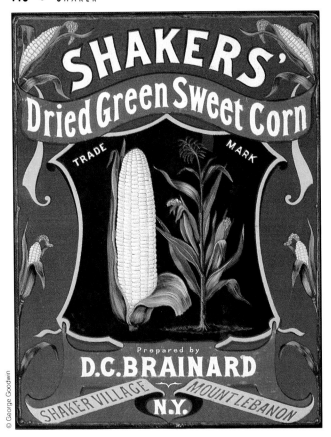

© George Goodwin

■ THIS EARLY SEED PACKET, OF A TYPE NOW FAMILIAR TO ALL GARDENERS, WAS A SHAKER INNOVATION THAT REVOLUTIONIZED THE SEED BUSINESS. THE ATTRACTIVE GRAPHIC QUALITY OF THE PACKET IS NOTABLE.

ALTHOUGH THE SHAKERS ARE KNOWN TODAY AS PURVEYORS OF AN ABUNDANCE OF GOOD THINGS TO eat, this was not always the case. The early Shakers under Mother Ann did not necessarily set a plentiful table; the lavish bounty of garden-fresh foods for which Believers later became famous simply was not yet available.

While the early communities were establishing their fundamental structure, with Believers busy clearing land and constructing buildings, mealtimes were abbreviated affairs. Accounts recall long periods in which basic fare was little more than bean soup, bread, and a little cider. These survival rations had to suffice in the wilderness that the Shaker pioneers were struggling to convert into farmland, largely with determination, since they had limited financial resources.

As Shaker communities moved west, these Believers met with similar hardship and faced the same lack of food. But the Shakers made heavenly order out of the chaos of the western frontier. They persevered through the trying times of their communities' developmental stages, to build and maintain farming facilities that produced food that not only met their own needs but those of the open market, as well.

As the nineteenth century progressed, Shaker farms grew large and prosperous. Believers learned to produce, in their prime years, virtually everything they needed in the way of food to support their large communities. There was an increasing variety of foodstuffs available as Shaker farming and livestock production became more sophisticated. The official monthly magazine of the Shakers, *The Manifesto,* ran regular features on food preparation, nutrition, and recipes.

Shaker agriculturalists were constantly augmenting the variety of their food production, planting new orchards, berry patches, and larger and more diversified gardens. Naturally, as the Shakers began growing additional types of fruits, vegetables, and grains, their diet became more varied. Accordingly, the Shaker sisters became bolder and more creative in their cooking, trying to utilize everything that was available. Whereas early Shaker cooking was the straightforward stuff of survival, Shaker sisters soon found themselves collecting and adapting recipes, as well as inventing new ones.

Those sisters whose primary responsibility was working in the kitchen did not hesitate to look outside their community for recipe ideas. By the mid-nineteenth century, sisters already had amassed collections of Shaker recipes that were looking more and more like cookbooks.

At the same time, Shaker cooking was assuming its own character, deviating more and more from ordinary New England country cooking. Shaker tables were open to innovation during their entire history, always receptive to new dishes and new means of preparation. A quick perusal of Shaker cookbooks is enough to establish that the Shaker diet was constantly evolving; at the same time it remained relatively simple.

Shaker cooks were nineteenth-century pioneers in canning fruits, vegetables, and meats for their own use, and for sale to the world. It is recorded that most communities produced huge quantities of canned goods efficiently and safely.

One for which the Shakers were particularly famous was their home-canned chicken. Several accounts indicate that this canned chicken had unparalleled flavor.

When processed white sugar became readily available in the mid-nineteenth century, there was a veritable explosion of fruit canning in some Shaker villages, with large amounts of goods sold to stores for use by the general population. At this time the Shakers began producing large amounts of candy for sale to the world, for which they soon became famous. Maple candy was a prized treat well into the twentieth century.

▲ FOOD PRODUCTION   Because of the Shaker belief that all tasks were a call to serve, it is not implausible that Believers regarded their kitchens nearly as highly as they did their meetinghouses. Eyewitnesses reported that Shaker sisters prepared delicious meals for their huge households without resentment, considering the responsibility not so much a chore as a true labor of love and a means of serving the Lord.

Courtesy The Winterthur Library: The Edward Deming Andrews Memorial Shaker Collection

■ SHAKER BROTHERS, IN THEIR ORGANIZED FASHION, USED HORSE POWER AND COMMUNAL EFFORT TO GRIND CORN INTO MEAL. THEIR SEEMINGLY FORMAL ATTIRE IS ACTUALLY WHAT THE BROTHERS WORE AS WORK CLOTHES.

Due to the vast quantities of food required in preparing a single meal, sisters had to perfect recipes to a science in order to have enough to feed everyone without incurring waste. In an age when most recipes were handed down verbally and cookbooks were a rare luxury, the Shakers developed methods of cooking that went beyond "a pinch of this and a dash of that"; sisters' cooking, like all other areas of Shaker life, became governed by precise and well-defined rules.

Shakers were encouraged to keep journals and diaries to account for their time and ideas. Consequently, we know a good deal more about their food preparation and eating habits than we do about those of their contemporaries. There is even a cookbook of early recipes by Shaker Sister Mary Witcher entitled, *The Shaker Housekeeper*.

In the Shakers' simple, ordered lives meals were a major event, and the type and quality of food were commented upon daily. The season's first raspberries or green beans, for example, were real occasions in the ordered round of Shaker lives, and they were special entries.

Shaker food was really just simple, well-prepared American country food, with much more attention to herbs and spices, quality of preparation, and eye-appeal than most country cooking of its period. The emphasis here, as in all things Shaker, was on simplicity. Shaker cooks were not *cordon bleu*, nor did they ever aspire to be. However, because Shaker sisters incorporated homegrown herbs and what, for that time, were considered to be exotic spices, Shaker cooking not only tasted good but was somewhat unique when compared to the general fare served on American tables of the time.

■ SIMPLE AND EFFICIENT, THIS FOOD PREPARATION AREA SHOWS THE SHAKERS' STYLISH, FUNCTIONAL WOOD BOWLS.

© Kenneth Martin/Amstock/Hancock Shaker Village, MA

▲ HEALTH FOOD

An interesting departure from the mass American taste in foods was the Shakers' brief but influential excursion into vegetarianism. A twelve-year ban on the use of meat started in the late 1830s and was followed throughout the whole Shaker world.

In contrast, American diets of the time were based upon the heavy use of meat, salt pork, and corn. Food was heavy, rich, and unhealthy, as well as overcooked. The Shaker diet, on the other hand, emphasized fresh and dried fruits, leafy green vegetables, eggs, cheese, and dairy products. This lighter, healthier regimen did not remain a secret to the outside world. To the contrary, the Shaker diet received wide exposure: Thousands of travelers were served meals at the Shaker settlements on their way west.

It would be misleading, however, to say that the vegetarian diet was universally accepted and enthusiastically embraced by Believers. The Shakers had their share of people who enjoyed meat. By way of compromise, for years the kitchens in many Shaker communities prepared separate menus—one for vegetarians and one for meat eaters.

The use of pork was strictly prohibited in Shaker kitchens for many years, and even nonvegetarians cooperated with this rule. It was probably wise, given poorly cooked pork's association with disease.

Gradually, meat returned to Shaker diets, but it was balanced by vegetables, fruit, and cereals. Even when vegetarianism had all but faded away and red meat was again in favor, the Shakers continued to rely heavily on their canned chickens. All in all, the vegetarian phase in Shaker culinary history was a positive step in making early nineteenth-century diets healthier and more well-balanced.

During the Shakers' health-food or vegetarian period, coffee, tea, liquor, and hard cider were more or less abandoned by Believers. Heavy use, or abuse, of these products was commonplace in early nineteenth-century America, and Shaker leaders were pioneers in seeking to control these substances. Alcohol never did return in any significant degree to the Shaker world, although Believers did produce a large variety of wines for "medicinal" purposes. Gradually tea and coffee were reintroduced, although all stimulants, like all foods—were taken only in moderation.

Overall, the Shakers can be viewed as having been revolutionary in their eating habits. They may have started the first major health-food movement in America, with lasting national effects on diet and health. The success of their dietary habits can be seen, even to the present day, in the extreme longevity and good health of many Shakers. It is amazing how many Shakers, from early days on, have lived into their high nineties, and beyond.

■ DIGNIFIED, AESTHETICALLY PLEASING GRAPHIC DESIGNS WERE USED ON CANS TO MARKET SHAKER GARDEN PRODUCE AND MEDICINAL PREPARATIONS.

▲ **AN HERBAL ART**   Among Shaker sisters' most significant innovations in the kitchen is their experimentation with herbs and spices. They were virtual pioneers in their time in the creative use of these ingredients.

Early in the nineteenth century, Believers were growing summer savory, sage, thyme, and sweet marjoram for their own use, as well as for sale to the outside world. Allspice, mace, and nutmeg were used in their kitchens, along with cayenne, mustard, and parsley. Extracts of almond, lemon, and vanilla found their way into Shaker foods, as did onion juice, celery, citron, raisins, and currants. The use of these simple and readily available herbs and spices lent real style and creativity to otherwise simple country cooking.

Without resorting to the elaborate and difficult-to-prepare sauces in the European gourmet tradition, Shaker cooks created healthy and practical dishes in which the natural mingling of juices, spices, and herbs created their own rich and special flavors. Some nineteenth-century visitors to Shaker dining rooms compared their fare with that of the finest New York restaurants.

■ THE HANDSOME SWEEP OF THE HERB GARDEN AT HANCOCK SHAKER VILLAGE IS A VIEW INTO THE EARLY NINETEENTH CENTURY; A VISION OF ORDER, BEAUTY, AND UTILITY.

© Jeff Greenberg/Hancock Shaker Village, MA

▲ VISUAL INTEREST

It seems to have been consistently important to Shaker sisters that their food not only taste good, but be attractive as well. Every recipe book and interview with sisters who worked in the kitchens indicate that a contrast of textures and colors on the plate was a goal of Shaker cooks.

Herbs such as parsley and marjoram certainly were used as flavorings, but their value went on to include the added color and visual interest they brought to a dish. Similarly, whether or not carrots were to be included in a menu might be dictated by the need for their color, as well as their availability.

This kind of culinary sensitivity was extremely unusual in nineteenth-century America. It was also a tradition handed down to future generations of Shaker sisters. Interviews with elderly Shaker sisters in this century indicated that among their first lessons in the kitchens, the sisters had been instructed on how to make food aesthetically pleasing.

Unlike Shaker architecture and furniture, which were aesthetically pleasing almost by happenstance, attractive meals were the result of deliberate efforts on the part of the Shakers. This perhaps can be attributed to the close association the Shakers made between food and God. To them, preparing and eating the bounty the Lord provided was another way to glorify God. The more attractive the food, the greater His glorification, it could be reasoned. Food was also a way to actively express a fundamental principle of Christianity—generous sharing with each other, and with the world. Almost any edible plant or grain available to the Shakers was seen as another example of God's bounty; consequently, it was used and shared in the best possible manner.

▲ MODEL KITCHENS

Shaker food was produced in some of the most pleasant, efficient kitchens available in nineteenth-century America. Their kitchens were large and well-lit, outfitted with beautiful and highly functional counters, work tables, and cupboards. Efficient and attractive storage was provided for every conceivable food item.

The Shakers' high premium on cleanliness naturally applied to the kitchen. These rooms were scrupulously clean, even when sisters were in the process of producing food for large groups. Late in the day the kitchens were scrubbed to gleaming perfection.

Almost all sisters worked in the kitchens in six- or eight-week periods, alternating with other types of work in the villages. Children, both boys and girls, were always in the kitchens as cooks' helpers—the girls doing odd jobs in preparation and cleaning, the boys fetching items and keeping the fires ablaze. The kitchens, pleasant and peaceful, seem to have been places in which most sisters enjoyed spending time.

■ A SAGE PLANTING IN THE HERB GARDEN AT HANCOCK SHAKER VILLAGE IS VISUALLY PLEASING TO VISITORS, ALTHOUGH LIKE ALL SHAKER PLANTINGS IT IS MEANT TO BE PURELY FUNCTIONAL.

The Shakers were constantly updating their kitchens with the most modern stoves and equipment—a testament to the importance of good cooking to Shakers, even in the years of their communities' decline in the twentieth century. Some real innovations occurred in Shaker kitchens. One, for example, was the revolving oven, which distributed heat evenly and efficiently, resulting in a variety of delicious baked goods. These ovens produced the famous Shaker baked beans, which in later days were widely marketed to the outside world.

Before the advent of gas and electric stoves, much of Shaker cooking was done in "arch kettles." These were all-purpose kettles that were hung on arched, swing-away brackets. They could do anything, from steaming puddings to making soups to preparing meats.

▲ DINING HABITS

Shaker meals were taken in silence at long tables in a long dining room. The sisters who cooked the meals also served the food, answering only in low whispers when something was requested. Meals were completed quickly, often in fifteen minutes or less. Eating silently helped quicken the meal.

Sisters sat at assigned tables on one side of the room, and brethren sat at separate assigned tables on the opposite side of the room. A small bell summoned the members of a family to meals. At its sound, they were to stop their work, form a procession in the hallway in their dining-room seating order, brothers first, and enter the dining hall in single file. Brothers and sisters, after arriving at their places at the table, said a blessing while standing next to their chairs, knelt for about two minutes, and then were signaled by an elder to rise and begin eating. This routine was mandated by Shaker law: "All should leave their work when the signal is given for them to gather in at mealtime, and be in their rooms in readyness to repair to the dining room, in order and in the fear of God, keeping step together."

Food was served family style, with the tables arranged in groups of four to avoid reaching; in every Shaker quartet, all food and condiments needed for the meal were available. When a platter or bowl was empty, sisters who were on kitchen duty quickly replaced them.

The completion of a meal followed much the same ritual as the beginning. When a meal was done, all arose silently at the request of an elder brother, knelt to pray and give thanks, and very quietly left the room in unison, returning to their appointed tasks.

▲ HOSPITALITY TO OUTSIDERS

People from outside the Shaker communities frequently visited them, many out of a curiosity to observe such a different way of life, others to experience a Shaker service. Whatever the reasons, outsiders found the Shakers welcoming, routinely opening their doors on the Sabbath.

© Kenneth Martin/Amstock/Hancock Shaker Village, MA

With these visits came the promise of dinner, and for that reason alone many of the worldly came to the Shakers' door. Shaker communities became famous for their food in the nineteenth century, and their dining rooms attracted many visitors. Some Shaker communities maintained separate dining rooms for visitors that were often more formal and elegant than regular Shaker dining rooms. These rooms would use better quality china, silver, linens, and glassware than normally seen in an austere Shaker dining room.

In early- and mid-nineteenth-century America, Shakers in the western communities served countless meals to strangers traveling west. Because of a great lack of food and hotels, Shaker hospitality was especially appreciated. In 1837 one guest recorded that the visitors were served a lunch that consisted of "delicious bread some wheaten some of corn, and some made of molasses; cheese, butter, spring water, and currant wine," adding that those who were lucky enough to share in the meal "could have gone on eating such bread and butter all day."

After the end of frontier times, Shakers continued to open their doors to strangers at mealtime. There are accounts of one Massachusetts community routinely expecting forty or more guests at one time from Boston.

■ SPARE, ELEGANT, AND EFFICIENT; THE SUPREMELY FUNCTIONAL DINING AREA AT HANCOCK SHAKER VILLAGE WAS A SERENE BACKGROUND FOR THE TASTY, SUPERB DINNERS.

Courtesy: The Winterthur Library: The Edward Deming Andrews Memorial Shaker Collection

■ THE NORTH FAMILY DINING ROOM AT NEW LEBANON, NEW HAMPSHIRE, IS SHOWN ARRANGED FOR DINNER WITH CAREFULLY PLANNED TABLES AND IMMACULATE SURROUNDINGS.

Shaker dining rooms, while always spartan in decor, were nonetheless attractive in their simplicity. The unadorned dishes and glassware matched, and the tables were attractively set. Numerous surviving photographs of late nineteenth-century dining rooms show the rooms to be carefully and elaborately decorated for holidays such as Christmas. It was important to the Shakers that their dining room chairs and tables were matched throughout, and that all the furnishings be comfortable and of good quality. Dining rooms, like virtually every other room in a Shaker building, generally had a good deal of practical built-in storage for dishes, glassware, and other necessities.

In addition to opening their dining halls to outsiders, the Shakers demonstrated hospitality in other ways. In their heyday of prosperity and healthy populations, Shaker communities had their kitchens sending out large quantities of food to the poor and needy. Shaker food was superior in cleanliness, taste, nutrition, and variety to the restaurant food of the period.

Later on, as some of the Shaker communities declined appreciably, they briefly functioned as boardinghouses. For instance, the community at Pleasant Hill, Kentucky, sold meals for forty or fifty cents a day, with room rent about the same.

It can be concluded that, from shortly after the beginning of the Shaker experience in America to the days of its decline, visitors from the outside world always were present at various times at Shaker dining tables, enjoying Believers' hospitality and good food. Even at the peak of Shaker prosperity, neighbors were invited regularly to dine with the Shakers for a nominal fee. These meals were called the World's People's Dinners and often constituted the major contact between Shakers and their neighbors.

Shaker food not only established a bond between communities and the world, it also was a drawing card in attracting a special breed of brethren. Although Shaker communities were fiercely regulated on the fine matters of daily life, they, oddly, had no rules about leaving the society. Each member was free to leave when he or she desired, with no repercussions or future ostracization. This freedom, when coupled with Shaker food, led to a group of Believers known as Winter Shakers. Mostly men, they would arrive at a Shaker community sometime in the late fall and remain through the winter months when the work load was light. Throughout the season, they could, of course, enjoy the sisters' exceptional food. Spring, with its greater workload, resulted in the Winter Shakers losing a bit of their religious convictions. They would leave the village, only to return the next year. Never admonished, some of these people returned year after year, like migrating birds. But then, considering the temptation of a fine Shaker meal, their motives are at least understandable.

© Kenneth Martin/Amstock/Hancock Shaker Village, MA

■ OLD-FASHIONED BAIL-TOP CANNING JARS HOLD THE BOUNTY OF SHAKER GARDENS AND KITCHENS.

FRESH
Garden Seeds.
United Socie W. GLOUCES UP BY West Gloucester, Me.
FOR SALE HRE.E.

SHAKERS GENUINE GARDEN SEEDS, MOUN LEB

SHAKERS GENUINE GARDEN SEEDS M LE

SHAKERS GENUINE GARDEN SEEDS

SHAKERS GENUINE GARDEN SEEDS

© Richard Day/Shakertown at South Union, KY

Chapter Six

▲▲▲

Gardens, Orchards, and Seed Industry

"If we toil diligently and improve faithfully
the talent given to us, and give liberally to
others the product of our labors, by this
means we can bless humanity and carry the
fruitage of a rich harvest to our own garners."

Sister Antoinette Doolittle, Mt. Lebanon

"The fruit of all hand labor is the true
service of God."

Elva F. Collins, Mt. Lebanon

"When we sow words and deeds
of kindness, we will rejoice in the time
of our harvest."

Larz Erickson, Pleasant Hill

(Quotes are from *A Collection of Shaker Thoughts*, by
Colin Becket, ed.)

© D. Long/Envision

■ FIELDS OF POPPIES, GROWN FOR MEDICINAL PURPOSES, MADE A BEAUTIFUL VISTA IN THE VILLAGE.

A GARDEN FOR ITS OWN SAKE WAS OF NO VALUE TO THE EVER-PRACTICAL SHAKERS. INSTEAD, A GAR-
den had to serve a purpose—either to produce food for the table or herbs for the care of the sick—for its existence to be justified.

This does not mean that Shaker grounds were devoid of flowers, however. Flowers abounded both within the confines of the village itself as well as in Shaker fields, but their purpose was not the bringing of mere pleasure via beautiful blossoms.

Roses, for example, were grown to make rosewater, a flavoring still used in baking today and which, at one time, was thought to reduce fever when bathed on the forehead. Sisters were forewarned not to make an idol of these flowers but, "in order that we might not be tempted to fasten a rose upon a dress or to put it in water to keep, the rule was that the flowers should be plucked with no stem at all," recalled one sister.

Entire fields of poppies were a part of many Shaker communities. Early in the morning, before breakfast, one could see sisters caped and cloaked against the morning dampness, slitting the seedheads of the poppies. Then again, in the late evenings, the women would return to the fields to collect sap from the plants that had dried during the day. This powdered sap was used to make medicinally valuable opium, a large cash crop for the Shakers.

As the nineteenth century drew to a close, the Shakers relaxed many of the rules governing their way of life. One of the rules that became more liberal was directed at the growing of flowers. Young girls living with the Shakers or who were sent to them for schooling were taught to tend flower beds, and sisters sometimes gathered a few blooms to enhance the dwellings. On the whole, however, the truly opulent gardens associated with the Victorian era never took root in the simplicity-oriented settlements of Shakers.

▲ **HERB GARDENS**   The use of herbs for medicinal purposes goes back practically to the beginning of time, with much of our knowledge of herb lore coming from the monasteries and cloisters of the Middle Ages. Since the inception of the first Shaker communities, the cultivation of herbs was an important aspect of life.

Shaker villages had a shortage of doctors, making a knowledge of the healing properties of herbs especially useful. Herbs also were valued in Shaker communities for the seasoning they provided to otherwise flavorless foods. Although the Shakers were not the first to grow herbs in the New World, they expanded their cultivation and transformed their usage into a science of sorts.

Much of the Shakers' knowledge about regional plants and their uses was gleaned from friendly neighboring Native Americans. Native roots, berries, and flowers introduced to the Shakers by the Native Americans were added to the Shaker gardens alongside the European and oriental herbs the Believers already were cultivating. The Shakers carefully explored the potential culinary and medicinal uses of virtually every weed, flower, and vegetable.

The poor, rocky New England soil served as a good medium for herb growth. Many of the herbs of Mediterranean origin require good drainage, full sun, and poor soil. Consequently, the Shakers had choice conditions for an herb garden industry.

▲ **CULINARY HERBS**   The Shakers grew several types of herbs, each for various uses. Cooking herbs were desirable for the flavor and appearance they added to food. The Shaker discovered that even the plainest and most bland foods could have mouthwatering appeal as a result of the culinary use of herbs.

This use of herbs was uncommon at the time. Rural New England cooking in the late eighteenth and early nineteenth centuries was less than appealing in both taste and appearance. With salt being the most common flavor enhancer at the time, the new herbal ingredients used by the Shakers established them as real innovators in the culinary arts. What modern cooks consider basic herbs—marjoram, thyme, basil, and summer savory—were anything but commonplace in North American cooking at that time. Yet Shaker sisters mixed these herbs together in various combinations for a seemingly infinite possibility of flavors, experimenting to avoid monotony in an otherwise simple diet. Naturally, some herbs were paired with certain foods more or less consistently—for instance, tarragon was paired with eggs; fennel and dill with fish; pork and poultry were infused with sage; lamb was spiced with marjoram and mint.

Other herbs grown for kitchen use included anise, several types of basil, parsley, caraway, chervil, coriander, oregano, rosemary, savory, and thyme. The Shakers also grew celery, not only for its stalk, but for its seeds and leaves, which served as seasonings.

The herb industry flourished for some time, but as the number of Shakers dwindled and more and more communities closed their doors, the growing of fine herbs also ebbed. The Shakers at Sabbathday Lake, however, revived their herb business in the 1970s. Keenly aware of the interest in fine cooking and a growing tourist trade, the village devoted a large portion of its land to the cultivation of culinary herbs. Today, these herbs, packaged in tins similar to the ones used by Shakers of an earlier era, are sold at the village store, at gourmet food shops, and through mail order.

© Kenneth Martin/Amstock/Hancock Shaker Village, MA

■ *OPPOSITE PAGE:* A STUDY IN BEAUTY AS A SIDE-EFFECT OF FUNCTION, THE LAUNDRY AND MACHINE SHOP BUILDING AT HANCOCK SHAKER VILLAGE. NOTICE THE HANDSOME WOOD DOOR. *ABOVE:* SHAKER BUILDINGS HAD MORE THAN ONE USE: HERE, HERBS ARE SEEN DRYING IN THE LAUNDRY AND MACHINE SHOP AT HANCOCK SHAKER VILLAGE.

© Kenneth Martin/Amstock/Hancock Shaker Village, MA

■ SHAKER PHARMACIES SUCH AS THIS ONE AT HANCOCK SHAKER VILLAGE, BROUGHT HERBAL HEALING TO AMERICA AND MONEY TO THE SHAKER COMMUNITIES.

▲ **MEDICINAL HERBS**   Healing herbs were extremely important to Shakers in their health care. Each village had at least one infirmary, and here the Shakers used their knowledge of herbs to treat assorted ailments.

The Shakers weren't stingy with their knowledge of herbal pharmacology. They shared their medicinal herbs with neighbors, and eventually, began marketing them on a broad scale to the "world." These sales became vastly important to the economy in some communities. The earliest recorded sale of medicinal herbs was in 1820, with families soon growing large amounts of herbs for commercial purposes.

The Shakers had some fortuitous assistance: A market for their herbs was created by a popular book, *The Guide to Health*. Written by Massachusetts herbalist and doctor, Samuel Thomson, the book presented a health program that relied heavily on herbal remedies.

By 1831 the herb trade at New Lebanon was sufficient enough to merit the production of a Shaker herb catalog. Printed in Albany, New York, it contained 120 different herbs, roots, and barks. The recorded sales from this first catalog were encouraging enough for the family to turn more land to the cultivation of herbs. Incredibly, sales were not only nationwide but international, with shipments going to London and Paris.

The herb industry had grown so much that, by the year 1856, a revised catalog was issued. Its title page read: "Catalog of Medicinal Plants, Barks, Roots, Seeds, Flowers, and Selected Powders; with their Therapeutic Qualities and Botanical Names; also Pure Vegetable Extracts, Prepared in Vacuo, Ointments, Inspissated Juices, Essential Oils, Doubled Distilled and Fragrant Waters, Etc. Raised, Prepared, and Put Up in the Most Careful Manner, by the United Society of Shakers in New Lebanon, N.Y." By 1855, herb production at New Lebanon had grown to seventy-five tons annually—an enormous amount, even for modern times. Records from other Shaker communities show that there, too, herb production was a significant industry, both in terms of size and profit.

The tracts of land devoted to medicinal herbs were known as "Psysic Gardens," and the medicinal herb cultivation itself was thought of as a "consecrated industry." Shakers, in other words, regarded it as their sacred duty to care for their own, and other people's health, by the means they knew best—herbal medicine.

Medicines were made from distillations of herbs, and came in a variety of forms—ointments, powders, liquids, and even pills. Many of these items found a ready market in the outside world. Cobertt's Syrup of Sarsaparilla made in the Shaker settlement at Canterbury, New Hampshire, was known nationwide as "The Great Purifier of the Blood and Other Fluids of the Body."

Whether or not all these herbal remedies were successful isn't as important as the fact that many of the Shaker products undoubtedly had some medicinal value. After all, the Shakers were extremely honest about business practices, and this extended to their medicinal claims and cures. This scrupulousness set the Shakers apart from the typical herbalists of the nineteenth century—an era of disreputable medicine men and snake-oil salesmen. Many of the concoctions hawked from wagons by these salesmen were nothing more than alcohol.

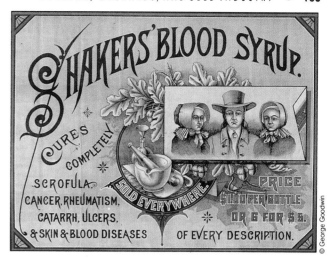

© George Goodwin

■ *ABOVE:* USING HERBS FROM THEIR OWN GARDENS THE SHAKERS WERE ABLE TO DEVISE ALL SORTS OF MEDICINES, INCLUDING THIS SHAKER BLOOD SYRUP. *BELOW:* THE CLOSE JUXTAPOSITION OF FAMILY DWELLINGS AT THE NEW LEBANON, NEW YORK, COMMUNITY, SHOWS HOW THOROUGHLY INTEGRATED THE VARIOUS ELEMENTS OF SHAKER LIFE WERE.

Courtesy The Winterthur Library: The Edward Deming Andrews Memorial Shaker Collection

Courtesy The Winterthur Library: The Edward Deming Andrews Memorial Shaker Collection

■ SISTER JENNIE MATHEWS, A PRIMLY DRESSED NINETEENTH-CENTURY SISTER, STANDS AMONG ENORMOUSLY TALL, PRE-HYBRID CORNSTALKS. SHAKERS WERE AMONG THE FIRST HYBRIDIZERS OF VEGETABLES.

Believers went to great lengths to ensure the purity of each herb distilled into a medicine. Large sheets and baskets were laid on the ground and only one type of herb was collected at a time. This harvest was then brought back to the herb house before the next type of herb was gathered. This process prompted a Yale professor to write in 1832: "They take great pains in packing their medicinal herbs, and so highly are they valued that they have frequent orders for them from Europe to a very large amount."

▲ KITCHEN GARDENS

Kitchen gardens were planted close to the family dwelling houses for ease and efficiency in bringing produce from the garden to table. These vegetable gardens were intended primarily for the feeding of the Shaker family and were distinctly apart from those devoted to the commercial seed and herb enterprises.

The proximity of the vegetable garden to the house ensured that only the freshest produce appeared on the Shaker tables. "A place for everything, and everything in its place" did not only refer to the interiors of Shaker dwellings. Millennial Laws required Believers to "lay out and fence all kinds of lots, fields and gardens, in square form, where it is practicable." Consequently, the Shakers grew a wide variety of vegetables and also experimented with the hybridization of many forms.

Much of the Shaker's wealth and wisdom came from a close communion with the land. As in all other Shaker endeavors, tending a garden was approached with a seriousness of purpose intended to please God. It was only natural that, given such care, Shaker grounds would yield with abundance. In their gardening, the Shakers invested an energy akin to that devoted to their spiritual lives, and, often, the two areas overlapped, each being held up as a metaphor for the other. It was not uncommon to hear comments such as this one from a Shaker brother: "If you would have a lovely garden, you should live a lovely life."

With the Shaker desire to improve on the raw materials granted them by God, it was not long before societies were developing methods to improve the produce they were growing, as well as, and in conjunction with, the methods by which they were grown and harvested. A labor-saving device was invented to distribute seeds during planting, for example. A ten-foot wooden seeder was filled with seed, and a cord was placed around its neck and balanced with a fitted waistband. The seeds were distributed by the turn of a lever that allowed them to drop in an even pattern a few at a time. The invention allowed one man to cover a wide expanse of land, saving the community time and manpower.

Another invention cut down on the amount of stooping and bending involved in planting large seeds such as corn, freeing up the community to spend more time worshipping God.

This labor saver was a tall, wooden V-shaped implement with a metal can attached to one side. When pressed into the soil, the handles were pulled apart, turning an orb inside the canister, which then lowered a kernel into the soil.

The Shakers were not opposed to adapting methods and machinery from the outside world in order to lighten and streamline their own workload. In a systematic fashion, brethren investigated, purchased, and improved upon implements such as seed separators and threshing machines. Such attention to efficiency paid off handsomely: Many Shaker journals tell of ample harvest—800 bushels of potatoes, 115 bushels of corn, 100 bushels of turnips, and four loads of pumpkins. This abundance far exceeded that of surrounding farms and can only be explained by the effort and ingenuity of the Shakers.

At the height of the Shaker movement, many acres were tilled to produce carrots, beets, parsnips, onions, celery, tomatoes, cucumbers, peas, spinach, cabbage, squash, and beans. Much of this was grown to feed Shaker families, but there also was a large and eager market awaiting surplus Shaker-grown produce.

▲ ORCHARDS

"The earth does not show more flourishing fields, gardens and orchards than theirs," wrote an observer of the nineteenth-century Shakers.

As with any large farm, the Shaker community featured orchards as an integral part of its agricultural production. Many acres were devoted to fruit trees set in neat, precise rows in characteristic Shaker fashion.

The most common tree grown in Shaker orchards was the apple tree. Several varieties of early apples were grown, with Pippen, Jonathan, and Ben Davis apples being the most widespread. At Sabbathday Lake, other varieties included Baldwin, Rhode Island, Greening, Red Astrachen, and Winter Banana.

Sister Frances A. Carr tells of the late Brother Delmer Wilson who tended the orchard at Sabbathday Lake until his eighty-ninth year. Early in this century Brother Delmer planted a new orchard with the idea of the village becoming a commercial apple grower. He planted row after row of the popular Red and Yellow Delicious, Cortland, and MacIntosh species, along with less commercial saplings of apples from almost extinct varieties.

Today, his orchard grows on a hilltop overlooking the Shaker community. Through the years, the apples thrived, providing gratification for Brother Delmer and becoming an attraction in themselves. The orchard's intrinsic beauty was responsible for its selection as the host site for the annual meetings of the Maine State Pomological Society's annual meetings. In late spring, the orchards are particularly spectacular. Sister Carr writes: "The white and pink

■ *TOP:* APPLE ORCHARDS WERE A MAJOR FEATURE OF ANY SHAKER COMMUNITY, AND THE BOUNTY OF THE DELICIOUS APPLE TREE IS IMPRESSIVE. *BOTTOM:* SHAKER FRUITS, VEGETABLES, AND MEDICINES WERE AMONG THE FIRST TO BE MARKETED WITH CAREFULLY CONCEIVED, EYE-CATCHING LABELS.

© George Goodwin

■ SHOWY, PICTORIAL LABELS WERE DESIGNED BY CANNY SHAKER ENTREPRENEURS TO MAKE ORDINARY ITEMS, SUCH AS THIS LAXATIVE CONTAINER (ABOVE) AND GREEN BEAN CAN LABEL (BELOW), DRAW CUSTOMER ATTENTION.

blooms are so thick they seem to cast a light over the area, and the scent of over 2,400 apple trees heavily laden with blossoms wafts down throughout the village, permeating all with its sweetness."

Brother Delmer's apple orchard was not only an aesthetic success, but a financial winner as well, bolstering the community's economy as a hardy industry. For the last twenty years of his life, Brother Delmer enjoyed driving the village truck to see the lovely location that he had devoted so much effort in creating. When at last it became inevitable that the aging man would not be able to maintain the orchard any longer, it was leased, and continues to be maintained by a neighboring orchardist. An agreement, however, does provide that the Shakers still be supplied with their fill of apples from it. As with all other Shaker enterprises, the orchard planted long ago by Brother Delmer remains a testament to the Believers' ability to combine utility and beauty.

But apples were only the beginning of the bounty that came from the well-tended grounds. Another important orchard crop was the cherry, grown to such an extent that, in May of 1872, the South Union family of Kentucky put up 3,941 jars of them. The early summer months through the first frost hosted a parade of fruits that included plums, peaches, quinces, and damsons, with pears and apples finishing out the harvest.

After being harvested, most of the fruit was dried or canned. That which wasn't used for family consumption was shipped to a vast market on the ever-expanding railway system. The orchard yields brought considerable income into the Shaker coffers, most notably in the southern communities of Kentucky, which had the longest growing season. Business records were kept of what was produced for the world's people, and, like all good marketing strategists, the Shakers promoted these household industries through advertising.

As with their herbs and vegetables, the Shakers established rules for the orchards. "Different species of trees, may not be engrafted or budded upon each other, as apples upon pears, quince, etc., peaches upon cherries, or contrary wise."

© George Goodwin

© George Goodwin

■ THIS SEED BOX LABEL IS ITSELF A WORK OF ART, AS WELL AS A COMMERCIAL INNOVATION.

▲ SEED INDUSTRY

The Shakers were the first mail-order seedsmen in America. They were the first to make an organized, efficient attempt at marketing seeds, and did so in a business-like, profitable manner. In the beginning, the commercial ventures were simple and local: Shakers actually traveled down the road to the nearest settlement, where they sold their seeds on consignment.

Brother James Holmes was the first official seedsman at Sabbathday Lake and, under his guidance, the industry flourished. The Shakers were relentless in seeking uniform, predictable quality and freshness in their seeds. Shaker seeds were not to be carried over from year to year, neither in the Shakers' own stock nor on a merchant's shelves.

The Shakers took great pride in their honesty—in being true to their word—and this standard applied to the goods they sold to the outside world. They wanted nothing to blemish their reputation for integrity. At the beginning of their seed industry, the Shakers included seed from local farmers to help fill orders. This, however, resulted in some dissatisfaction among the customers the Shakers were trying to please. The situation was intolerable. In 1819, the Believers ensured customer satisfaction by guaranteeing the contents of each seed pack to be entirely Shaker-grown. This pact was agreed upon by the communities of Hancock, New Lebanon, and Watervliet. Called an "Ancient Witness", it stated: "We, the undersigned, having for some time past felt a concern, lest there should come some loss upon the joint interest, and dishonor upon the gospel, by purchasing seeds of the world, and mixing them with ours for sale; and having duly considered the matter, we are confident that it is best to leave off the practice, and we do hereby convenant and agree that we will not, hereafter, put up, or sell, any seeds to the world which are not raised among Believers (except mellon seeds)."

By the mid-nineteenth century the sight of a Shaker brother in his seed wagon going up and down the farm roads in springtime was familiar in much of rural New England. Seeds were brought to stores on consignment, and at the end of the season the Shakers would return to collect their money and any remaining inventory. This ensured that there would be no leftover, stale seeds in the stores the following spring to give Shaker seeds a bad name with farmers and gardeners. From its small-scale origins, the seed industry grew into a large and significant economic resource for most of the Shaker communities.

During peak growing and harvesting season many members of a family might be engaged in the production and sale of seeds. The gardeners, of course, raised the seeds, and seedpersons culled and sorted them. There was also considerable correspondence carried on all year by the office deacons concerning the sales, orders, and the production of seed catalogs. Seed boxes were made by Shaker carpenters; printers made the labels and later printed their own catalogs. Sisters cut and pasted the seed bags together and were the chief seed sorters.

As early as 1826, the list of seeds for sale was extensive. It included Early Petersburg, Large White Marrowfat, and two other varieties of peas; two kinds of beet—blood and turnip; and three species of onion—red, yellow, and white.

To larger retail and wholesale customers, the Shakers sold at wholesale prices; often sales to smaller customers were on commission. As both production and the market grew, the Shakers devoted a good part of their seed business to mail orders.

In marketing their seed products, the Shakers developed a real innovation: the individual paper seed packet. They not only invented the seed pack as we know it today, but also the

■ SHAKER SEED LISTS OFFER A GLIMPSE INTO NINETEENTH-CENTURY GARDENING AND CULINARY HABITS, AND WERE, FOR THE TIME, EXTRAORDINARILY VARIED.

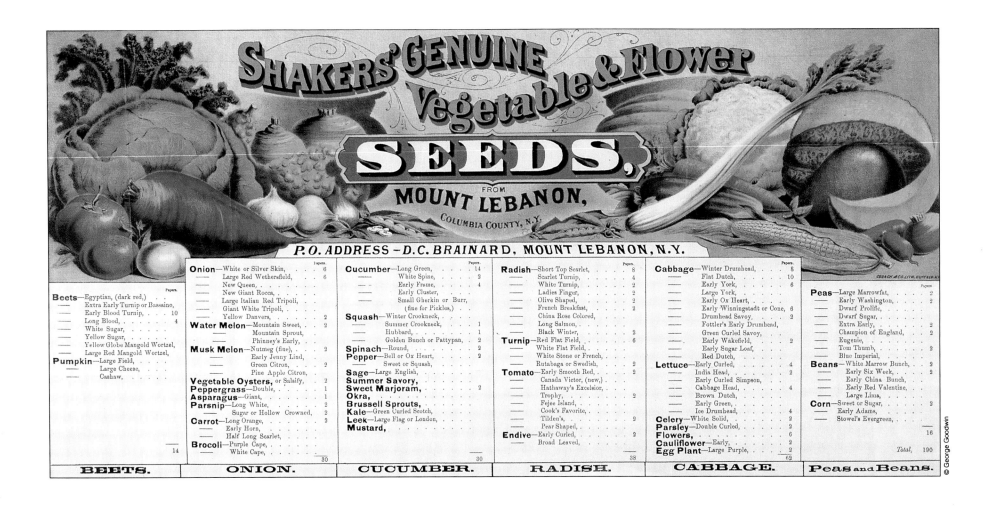

machines that cut the packets, printed them, and filled them with seed. At first the Shakers designed and printed individual seed packets with the expected Shaker simplicity of style, in order to market carefully and efficiently small quantities of garden seed. Later in the century they designed and printed brightly colored posters advertising their seeds, and the seed packets, accordingly, were colorfully illustrated. Although the development of the seed packet is an often overlooked innovation of the Shakers, it revolutionized the seed business, and, indeed, set it on its present course. Those early, simple paper seed packets, of which few have survived, are now highly prized by collectors.

Every New York and New England Shaker community became involved in the seed business, and some feelings of competition ensued between the communities. Each family set up definite and specific areas as their exclusive sales territories and they did not relish their fellow brethren trespassing into their seed sales regions. As shrewd businessmen, they engaged in comparative analysis of regions, according to their populations. For instance, a sparsely populated area meant that the Shaker community purveying it with seed would require a larger geographic territory than a Shaker group servicing a more concentrated urban population.

The Shakers' development and organization of the seed business, coupled with their standardization of seed quality, made an incalculable difference to pioneering American farmers and gardeners. Thanks to the Shaker seed business, virtually all frontier American farmers and gardeners could rely upon dependable, quality seeds to be available by mail or at retail every year. In turn, the Shakers' high-quality strains of vegetable seeds made a favorable impact on our nation's diet.

Many Shaker seed catalogs included simple instructions on how to plant and grow a vegetable garden successfully. This, too, served an important function in facilitating a greater use of vegetables in the American diet by simplifying the growing process and reducing the likelihood of failure. The mail-order aspect of the Shaker seed business meant that citizens in remote, frontier areas had the broad variety of Shaker vegetables and herbs available to them, and should they not know how to grow them, the Shakers' printed instructions on the packets would teach them.

The Shaker seed business eventually met with outside competition, and the families went out of the business. Probably a major factor in the decline of the Shaker seed business was the declining Shaker population, as the pool of workers for this labor-intensive business grew smaller and smaller. Nevertheless, the impact of Shaker innovation in the business is evident even today, long after most Shaker families are gone.

© Richard Day/Shakertown at South Union, KY

■ THIS INTERESTING CONTRAPTION IS A SHAKER SEED CLEANER. THE SHAKERS DEVELOPED THE TECHNOLOGY AND EQUIPMENT TO MAKE A MASS SEED BUSINESS SUCCESSFUL.

KITCHEN METRICS

▲▲▲

▲ SPOONS

¼ teaspoon = 1 milliliter

½ teaspoon = 2 milliliters

1 teaspoon = 5 milliliters

1 tablespoon = 15 milliliters

2 tablespoons = 25 milliliters

3 tablespoons = 50 milliliters

▲ CUPS

¼ cup = 50 milliliters

⅓ cup = 75 milliliters

½ cup = 125 milliliters

⅔ cup = 150 milliliters

¾ cup = 175 milliliters

1 cup = 250 milliliters

▲ OVEN TEMPERATURES

200°F = 100°C	350°F = 180°C
225°F = 110°C	375°F = 190°C
250°F = 120°C	400°F = 200°C
275°F = 140°C	425°F = 220°C
300°F = 150°C	450°F = 230°C
325°F = 160°C	475°F = 240°C

■ ANOTHER EXAMPLE OF SHAKER SKILL IN MARKETING OF THEIR FRUIT, VEGETABLE, AND MEDICINAL PRODUCTS, THIS LABEL IS PARTICULARLY ATTRACTIVE AND STYLISH.

© George Goodwin

BROTHER WAYNE'S APPLESAUCE CAKE

▲▲▲

- ▲ 2½ CUPS FLOUR
- ▲ 1¾ CUPS BROWN SUGAR
- ▲ ½ TEASPOON BAKING POWDER
- ▲ 1½ TEASPOONS BAKING SODA
- ▲ 1 TEASPOON SALT
- ▲ 1 TEASPOON CINNAMON
- ▲ ½ TEASPOON CLOVES
- ▲ ½ TEASPOON ALLSPICE
- ▲ ½ TEASPOON NUTMEG
- ▲ ½ TEASPOON GINGER
- ▲ ½ CUP SHORTENING
- ▲ 1¾ CUPS APPLESAUCE
- ▲ 3 EGGS
- ▲ 1 CUP RAISINS
- ▲ 1 CUP NUTS, CHOPPED (OPTIONAL)

Sift flour, sugar, baking powder, baking soda, salt, and spices together. Add shortening and applesauce and beat just enough to combine. Add in eggs and beat until well combined. Fold in the raisins and nuts. Pour into a greased and floured 13" x 9" x 2" baking pan. Bake at 350° for 45 minutes or until a tester inserted in the center comes out clean.

SHAKER APPLE PIE

▲▲▲

- ▲ 3 CUPS APPLES, PEELED AND SLICED
- ▲ ⅔ CUP SUGAR
- ▲ 1 TABLESPOON CREAM
- ▲ 1 TABLESPOON SHAKER ROSE WATER
- ▲ PASTRY FOR TWO 9-INCH CRUSTS

Slice apples into mixing bowl and add the sugar, cream, and rose water. Mix thoroughly so that the rose water will be distributed evenly. Line a pie dish with pastry. Fill with the apple mixture and cover with top crust in which a few small vents have been slashed for steam to escape. Brush with a very little rose water mixed with milk. Bake in a moderate oven, 350°, for 50 minutes.

THE FOLLOWING RECIPES ARE FROM: *Shaker Your Plate: Of Shaker Cooks and Cooking*, Sister Frances A. Carr, Sabbathday Lake, Maine: United Society of Shakers, 1986.

© Dick Luria/FPG International

■ APPLE PIE IS A TRADITIONAL AMERICAN—AND SHAKER—FAVORITE. THIS RECIPE REPRESENTS AMERICAN COUNTRY COOKING AT ITS BEST.

SISTER MARIE'S APPLE PIE
▲▲▲

- ▲ 6 LARGE APPLES
- ▲ 1 ¼ CUPS SUGAR
- ▲ ¼ TEASPOON NUTMEG
- ▲ ½ TEASPOON CINNAMON
- ▲ PASTRY FOR TWO 9-INCH CRUSTS

Peel and cut apples into thin slices. Layer the apples in a pastry-lined 9-inch pie plate. After using approximately half the apples, use half of the sugar and spices, sprinkling them over the apples. Fill with remaining apples and top with remaining sugar and spices. Top with small dots of butter. Add top crust and seal well. Make vents in top of pie for steam to escape. Bake for 15 minutes at 425°. Reduce heat to 350°. Continue baking for 40–45 minutes. Test apples for doneness.

SISTER MARIE'S PIE CRUST
▲▲▲

- ▲ 1 CUP VEGETABLE SHORTENING OR LARD
- ▲ 2½ CUPS FLOUR
- ▲ 1 TEASPOON SALT
- ▲ 4–5 TABLESPOONS COLD WATER

Sift the flour and salt together. Mix in the shortening until the pieces are the size of peas. Gradually add the cold water, 1 tablespoon at a time. Do not mix too much. Roll out onto a lightly floured board.

MAKES ENOUGH FOR TWO 9-INCH CRUSTS.

SISTER MARIE'S WHOLE WHEAT BREAD

▲▲▲

- ▲ 1 CUP MILK
- ▲ 2 TABLESPOONS SUGAR
- ▲ 2 TEASPOONS SALT
- ▲ ¼ CUP BUTTER OR MARGARINE
- ▲ 1½ CUPS WARM WATER
  (TEMPERATURE OF 105°–115°)

- ▲ ½ CUP MOLASSES
- ▲ 2 PACKAGES DRY ACTIVE YEAST
- ▲ 2½ CUPS SIFTED ALL-PURPOSE FLOUR
- ▲ 5 CUPS *UNSIFTED* WHOLE WHEAT FLOUR
- ▲ 2 TABLESPOONS MELTED BUTTER OR MARGARINE

Heat milk until bubbles form around the pan; remove from heat. Add the sugar, salt, butter, and molasses. Stir until butter melts. In a large bowl sprinkle the yeast over water and stir until dissolved. Stir in the milk mixture. Add all-purpose flour and 2½ cups of whole wheat flour. Beat with wooden spoon (if you have one) until smooth, about 4 minutes. Gradually add remaining whole wheat flour, mixing in the last of it with your hand, until the dough leaves the sides of the bowl.

Turn dough out onto a lightly floured board and allow to rest for 10 minutes. Knead until smooth, about 10 or 12 minutes. Kneading is very important for good bread so do not neglect it. Place dough in a greased bowl and turn the dough so as to bring greased side up. Cover with a light towel and let rise in a warm place away from drafts until dough doubles in bulk, about 1¼ hours. A good test is to poke 2 fingers into the dough and if the indentation remains the dough is ready. Punch down dough with hands. Turn dough out onto lightly floured board, divide in half and shape each half into a smooth ball. Let rest for 10 minutes. Shape each portion into a loaf and place in lightly greased 9 x 5 loaf pans. Cover with a towel and let rise in warm place until double in bulk or until the dough reaches the tops of the pans. This takes approximately 1½ hours.

Preheat oven to 400°. Bake loaves 40–45 minutes. The tops should be browned and sound hollow when rapped with knuckles. Remove bread from pans immediately and let cool.

MAKES TWO 9 x 5-INCH LOAVES.

© Michael Keller/FPG International

■ ANOTHER TEMPTING STAPLE OF THE SHAKER TABLE, THIS RICH, FULL-BODIED WHEAT BREAD IS A MEAL IN ITSELF.

© Dennis Gottlieb

■ THESE HERB-CHEESE ROLLS USE SHAKER-GROWN HERBS TO MAKE AN UNUSUAL TREAT. SHAKERS CONSTANTLY EXPERIMENTED WITH HERBS TO ENLIVEN THEIR COOKING.

HERB-CHEESE ROLLS
▲▲▲

- ▲ ½ CUP VERY WARM WATER
- ▲ 2 PACKAGES YEAST
- ▲ 1½ CUPS WARM WATER
- ▲ 1 TABLESPOON SUGAR
- ▲ 2 TEASPOONS SALT
- ▲ 5 CUPS SIFTED FLOUR

- ▲ ½ CUP GRATED PARMESAN CHEESE
- ▲ ½ CUP SHAKER PARSLEY
- ▲ 1 TEASPOON SHAKER OREGANO
- ▲ 1 TEASPOON SHAKER BASIL
- ▲ 1 EGG WHITE
- ▲ 1 TABLESPOON WATER

Pour very warm water into a large bowl. Sprinkle in yeast and stir until yeast is dissolved. Add the remaining water, sugar, salt, and 2½ cups of the flour. Beat together until well mixed. Stir in the remaining flour and mix until smooth. Knead the dough on a lightly floured board. Knead for 5 minutes. Turn into a greased bowl, cover, and let rise in a warm place until doubled in bulk, about 30 minutes. Meanwhile, combine the cheese with the parsley, oregano, and basil. Punch down the dough and divide in half.

Roll one half on a floured board to make a 9 x 5-inch rectangle. Spread dough with melted butter and sprinkle with herb-cheese mixture. Roll up dough jelly-roll style so that the roll is 15 inches long. Cut into 1-inch slices. Place in greased muffin tins, seam side down. Repeat with the remaining dough. Cover and rise until double in bulk, about 30 minutes. Bake in a 400° oven for 15 minutes.

Remove from oven. Brush with egg white that has been beaten with the water. Return to oven and bake for 10 minutes longer. Cool on wire racks for crispiness.

YIELDS 2½ DOZEN ROLLS.

TOMATO DILL SOUP

▲▲▲

- ▲ 1 TEASPOON BUTTER OR MARGARINE
- ▲ 1 TEASPOON FLOUR
- ▲ 2½ CUPS TOMATO PUREE
- ▲ ½ TEASPOON BAKING SODA

- ▲ 2 TEASPOONS SHAKER DILL
- ▲ SALT TO TASTE
- ▲ 5 CUPS HOT MILK
- ▲ ½ CUP SOUR CREAM (OPTIONAL)

In a medium size soup kettle melt the butter. Stir in the flour and cook for several minutes. Add tomato puree, dill, and salt. Stir in the baking soda. Simmer for 30 minutes. Heat milk and slowly stir into the sour cream. Add milk mixture to tomato mixture. Heat, stirring constantly, until hot.

HEARTY BEEF AND VEGETABLE SOUP

▲▲▲

- ▲ 3–4 POUND SOUP BONE OR BEEF SHANK
- ▲ 1 TEASPOON SALT
- ▲ 1 BAY LEAF
- ▲ ½ CUP DICED CELERY
- ▲ 1½ CUPS DICED POTATOES

- ▲ 1½ CUPS DICED CARROTS
- ▲ ½ CUP DICED TURNIP
- ▲ 3 MEDIUM ONIONS, CHOPPED INTO LARGE CHUNKS
- ▲ ½ TEASPOON *Bouquet Garni*

In large kettle combine bone or shank, salt, bay leaf, celery, and 1½ cups water. Bring to a boil and reduce heat to simmer. Cover and cook for 1½ hours or until the meat is tender.

Remove shanks and allow them to cool slightly. Skim fat off surface and cut meat from bones into small pieces approximately 1 inch long. Set meat aside.

In the stock combine all vegetables and bring to a boil. Reduce heat and allow to simmer for approximately 20 minutes or until potatoes, carrots, and turnips are almost tender. Add meat and continue simmering until all the vegetables are tender. Do not allow the meat to boil as it will grow stringy. Just before serving add ½ teaspoon Shaker Bouquet Garni and serve very hot with herb biscuits.

© Steven Mark Needham/Envision

■ SIMPLE TO PREPARE, ATTRACTIVE TO BEHOLD, AND A DELICIOUS VARIANT TO TOMATO SOUP, TOMATO DILL SOUP REPRESENTS ANOTHER CREATIVE WAY TO USE GARDEN HERBS.

The following recipe is from: *The Shaker Cookbook: Recipe & Lore from the Valley of God's Pleasure*, Caroline Piercy and Arthur Tolve.

The following recipes are from: *We Make You Kindly Welcome: Recipes From the Trustees' House Daily Fare*, Pleasant Hill, Kentucky.

■ THE BASIS FOR MANY HEARTY SHAKER DISHES SUCH AS FRIED APPLES, THESE RIPE BURGUNDY APPLES ON A TREE IN UPSTATE NEW YORK TANTALIZE THE EYE AND TASTE BUDS.

MAPLE CREAMS
▲▲▲

- ▲ 3 CUPS BROWN SUGAR
- ▲ 1 CUP CREAM
- ▲ 1½ TEASPOON MAPLE FLAVORING
- ▲ 1 CUP CHOPPED PECANS OR WALNUTS

In a saucepan, cook sugar and cream until a soft ball is formed when dropped into cold water. Remove from heat. Beat until very creamy and candy has cooled somewhat. Add maple flavoring. Butter a large platter and sprinkle with nuts. Pour candy over nuts and let cool. Cut into squares and store covered, in a cool, dry place.

Variation: These candies may be dipped into melted semi-sweet chocolate to coat. Let drain on a cooling rack over wax paper.

FRIED APPLES
▲▲▲

- ▲ 2 QUARTS SMALL TART APPLES
- ▲ ⅓ BOX LIGHT BROWN SUGAR
- ▲ 1 PINCH OF CINNAMON
- ▲ ⅓ STICK BUTTER OR MARGARINE

Cut unpeeled apples in six wedges from core to stem; remove the seeds. Place the apples in a skillet; sprinkle them with sugar and cinnamon, and dot with butter.

Cover the skillet with a lid or foil; place it on a cold stove. Set at low heat and cook until tender, stirring only occasionally. Remove the lid and cook 3 to 5 minutes longer.

BAKED ACORN SQUASH

▲▲▲

- ▲ 1 MEDIUM ACORN SQUASH
- ▲ MELTED BUTTER
- ▲ ¼ TEASPOON SALT
- ▲ ¼ TEASPOON CORN SYRUP (OR MIXTURE OF BROWN AND WHITE SUGAR)

Scrub squash. Cut in half lengthwise; scrape out seeds and stringy portion with spoon. Brush cut surface of each half with a little melted butter. Sprinkle each half with salt, ⅛ teaspoon to each half. Arrange, cut side down, in a baking pan. Bake in moderate oven 400° for 30 minutes. Then turn, cut side up, and brush well with butter mixed with corn syrup. Bake until tender, about 30 minutes. Brush often with syrup-butter mixture.

CHEESE CASSEROLE

▲▲▲

- ▲ 4 SLICES OF BREAD
- ▲ 2 SLICES OF CHEESE
- ▲ SALT AND PEPPER
- ▲ BUTTER
- ▲ 2 CUPS MILK
- ▲ 3 WELL-BEATEN EGGS
- ▲ DASH OF TABASCO

Butter bread and make cheese sandwiches. Butter baking dish and place sandwiches in the bottom, cutting them to fit your casserole.

Mix eggs and milk together, beating well; add seasonings; pour mixture over sandwiches. Let stand at least 3 hours in refrigerator. Sprinkle a little grated cheese on top. Bake at 325° for 1 hour.

GLAZED CARROTS

▲▲▲

- ▲ 1 QUART CANNED CARROTS
  (SMALL BELGIUM CARROTS ARE BEST)
- ▲ 2 TABLESPOONS BUTTER
- ▲ ½ CUP BROWN SUGAR

Drain the carrots. Place them in a baking dish, sprinkle with sugar, and dot with butter. Bake at 450° for about 20 minutes.

If fresh carrots are used, pare, boil until tender, then proceed as above.

© Steven Mark Needham/Envision

■ SQUASH IS A TRUE AMERICAN FOOD, MUCH APPRECIATED BY SHAKER COOKS.

■ FRESH GARDEN BEETS CAN STILL BE SEEN IN SURVIVING SHAKER GARDENS. THIS SHAKER BEET RECIPE IS A FRESH LOOK AT AN OLD FAVORITE.

BEST BEETS
▲▲▲

- ▲ 1 SMALL ONION, THINLY SLICED
- ▲ 1 TABLESPOON PLUS 1 TEASPOON BUTTER
- ▲ 1 TABLESPOON LEMON JUICE
- ▲ 1 TEASPOON CHOPPED PARSLEY
- ▲ 1 CAN BEETS
- ▲ ¼ TEASPOON SALT

Sauté onion lightly in butter until soft but not brown. Drain beets and place them in onion and butter. Add lemon juice and parsley. Toss beets, adding salt. Heat until hot.

SWEET PICKLES AND ONIONS
▲▲▲

- ▲ 6 QUARTS SLICED CUCUMBERS
- ▲ 5 CUPS SUGAR
- ▲ 1 TABLESPOON CELERY SEED
- ▲ 6 SLICED ONIONS
- ▲ ½ CUP MUSTARD SEED
- ▲ 1 TEASPOON TURMERIC
- ▲ SALT WATER
- ▲ 1 ¼ QUARTS CIDER VINEGAR

Slice onions and cucumbers. Cover with salt water and allow it to stand for 3 hours. Drain. Place sugar, mustard seed, celery seed, and turmeric in vinegar. Bring spices and vinegar to a boil. Place in sterilized jars, seal, and process.

CUCUMBER PICKLE
▲▲▲

- ▲ 5½ POUNDS RIPE YELLOW CUCUMBERS
- ▲ TURMERIC
- ▲ 1 TABLESPOON WHOLE CLOVES
- ▲ MUSTARD SEED
- ▲ 1 QUART VINEGAR
- ▲ 3½ TO 4 CUPS SUGAR
- ▲ 3 OR 4 CINNAMON STICKS

Peel, seed, and cut up cucumbers. Put in one gallon of lime water and let stand overnight. Drain. Wash through two or three waters. Put in kettle with vinegar and sugar and allow to come to a boil for a few minutes; then add cloves, mustard seed, cinnamon sticks; add turmeric for color. Let boil until pickles take yellow color; then strain off syrup. Pack sterilized jars with pickles. Boil syrup until it thickens a little; pour it over the pickles, seal, and process.

SHAKER SPICED APPLE CIDER

▲▲▲

- ▲ 3 QUARTS CIDER
- ▲ 1 STICK CINNAMON
- ▲ 1 WHOLE NUTMEG
- ▲ 1 WHOLE CLOVE
- ▲ ½ CUP SUGAR

Place spices in cheesecloth bag. Put cider, sugar, and bag in pan and simmer for at least 3 minutes. Serve hot in warmed cups.

BISQUE OF GARDEN PEA

▲▲▲

- ▲ 3 CUPS FRESH PEAS, OR FROZEN
- ▲ 2 CUPS WATER
- ▲ PINCH OF SALT
- ▲ ¼ CUP ONIONS, CHOPPED
- ▲ 3 TABLESPOONS BUTTER
- ▲ 3 TABLESPOONS ALL-PURPOSE FLOUR
- ▲ 3 CUPS MILK OR HALF-AND-HALF
- ▲ SALT AND RED PEPPER TO TASTE

Cook fresh peas in water with pinch of salt until tender, or according to directions on box of frozen peas. Cool slightly. Put peas, liquid, and onions in electric blender, blend until smooth. In large saucepan melt butter and stir in flour until smooth and bubbly. Remove from heat and stir in milk slowly. Return to low heat stirring constantly and cook until sauce thickens. Add puréed pea mixture and stir until blended. Season to taste with red pepper and salt. Chill until ready to serve. Garnish with chopped mint leaves.

MAPLE SYRUP FROSTING

▲▲▲

- ▲ 1 CUP MAPLE SYRUP
- ▲ 2 EGG WHITES, UNBEATEN
- ▲ ¼ TEASPOON SALT
- ▲ ½ CUP BLACK WALNUTS, HICKORY NUTS, OR PECANS, CHOPPED

Cook maple syrup to 240°–248° on candy thermometer or until a firm ball forms when dropped into cold water. Pour syrup slowly into egg whites beating all the time. Add salt and beat until thick. Frost cake and sprinkle nuts on top of frosting.

THE FOLLOWING RECIPES ARE FROM: *WELCOME BACK TO PLEASANT HILL: MORE RECIPES FROM THE TRUSTEES' HOUSE*, PLEASANT HILL, KENTUCKY.

© Steven Mark Needham/Envision

■ A CHILLED GREEN PEA SOUP, USING SIMPLE INGREDIENTS FROM THE SHAKER LARDER, WOULD BE A REAL TREAT ON A WARM SUMMER DAY.

■ RIPE RED PLUM TOMATOES FRESHLY GATHERED IN A GARDEN BASKET FORM THE BASIS FOR MANY OF THE GOOD SHAKER COUNTRY DISHES.

TOMATO OKRA CASSEROLE
▲▲▲

- ▲ 6 TABLESPOONS ONIONS, CHOPPED
- ▲ 2 TABLESPOONS BACON GREASE
- ▲ 1 POUND OKRA, SLICED
- ▲ 1 QUART TOMATOES, PEELED AND COOKED, OR CANNED
- ▲ ¼ TEASPOON CURRY POWDER
- ▲ ½ TEASPOON PAPRIKA
- ▲ 1 TABLESPOON SUGAR
- ▲ 1½ TEASPOONS SALT
- ▲ ¼ TEASPOON RED PEPPER
- ▲ 2½ TABLESPOONS PARMESAN CHEESE
- ▲ 8 BUTTER CRACKERS, CRUMBLED

Sauté onions in bacon grease. Add okra and cook until tender. Add tomatoes and seasoning. Pour in greased casserole dish. Top with cheese, then cracker crumbs. Bake at 350° for 35 minutes. Serves about twelve.

PLEASANT HILL CHRISTMAS CAKE
▲▲▲

- ▲ 3 CUPS ALL-PURPOSE FLOUR, SIFTED
- ▲ 3 TEASPOONS BAKING POWDER
- ▲ ¼ TEASPOON SALT
- ▲ ¾ CUP BUTTER
- ▲ 1½ CUPS GRANULATED SUGAR
- ▲ 1 CUP MILK
- ▲ 1 TEASPOON VANILLA
- ▲ 3 EGG WHITES, BEATEN UNTIL STIFF
- ▲ ½ CUP BLACK WALNUTS, HICKORY NUTS, OR PECANS, CHOPPED

Sift flour, baking powder, and salt together. Cream butter and sugar until very light. Add alternately flour and milk. Stir in vanilla. Fold in egg whites and then nuts. Pour into two greased and lightly floured eight-inch cake pans. Bake at 350° for about 30 minutes. Frost with Maple Syrup Frosting.

RHUBARB STRAWBERRY COBBLER

▲▲▲

- ▲ ½ CUP ALL-PURPOSE FLOUR
- ▲ 3 CUPS GRANULATED SUGAR
- ▲ 1 TEASPOON SALT
- ▲ 6 CUPS RHUBARB, SLICED
- ▲ 2 CUPS STRAWBERRIES, SLICED ONCE IF LARGE
- ▲ 4 TABLESPOONS BUTTER
- ▲ 1 TABLESPOON LEMON JUICE
- ▲ 1 9-INCH PIE CRUST, UNBAKED

Butter lightly 9 x 13 inch pan. Combine flour, sugar, and salt. Sprinkle over rhubarb and strawberries, and toss well. Heap mixture into greased pan and spread. Sprinkle with lemon juice and dot with butter. Top with pie crust; prick crust or cut slits in it. Bake at 450° for one hour.

KENTUCKY PIE

▲▲▲

- ▲ 1 UNBAKED 9-INCH PIE CRUST
- ▲ ¼ CUP BUTTER
- ▲ 1 CUP GRANULATED SUGAR
- ▲ 3 EGGS, BEATEN
- ▲ ¾ CUP WHITE CORN SYRUP
- ▲ ¼ TEASPOON SALT
- ▲ 1 TEASPOON VANILLA
- ▲ ½ CUP CHOCOLATE MORSELS
- ▲ ½ CUP CHOPPED NUTS
- ▲ 2 TABLESPOONS BOURBON

Cream butter and add sugar gradually. Add beaten eggs, syrup, salt, and vanilla. Add chocolate morsels, nuts, and bourbon. Stir until well mixed. Pour into pie crust and bake at 375° for 40 to 50 minutes. If crust browns rapidly, cover with foil or brown paper. Rewarm to serve. Serves seven or eight.

© Lynn Karlin

■ FRESH RHUBARB, RED AND TART, IS A SURE SIGN OF SPRING IN ANY GARDEN. THIS COBBLER IS A DELICIOUS SHAKER VARIATION ON AN OLD FAVORITE.

▲ SOURCES

▲ MAGAZINES

Shaker Spirit
Point Publishing Co., Inc.
P.O. Box 1309
Point Pleasant, NJ 08742

The Shaker Messenger
The World of Shaker
P.O. Box 1645
Holland, MI 49422-1645

▲ BOOKS

Carr, Sister Frances A. *Shaker Your Plate: Of Shaker Cooks and Cooking.* Sabbathday Lake, Maine: United Society of Shakers, 1986.

Kremer, Elizabeth C. *We Make You Kindly Welcome: Recipes From the Trustees' House Daily Fare.* Harrodsburg, Kentucky: Pleasant Hill Press, 1970.

——. *Welcome Back to Pleasant Hill: More Recipes From the Trustees' House.* Harrodsburg, Kentucky: Pleasant Hill Press, 1977.

Piercy, Caroline and Arthur Tolvy. *The Shaker Cookbook: Recipes & Lore from the Valley of God's Pleasure.* Bowling Green, Ohio: Gabriel's Horn Publishing Co., 1984.

Check bookshops at operating Shaker villages for a list of their inventory.

Others: Write *Shaker Spirit* or *The Shaker Messenger* (see addresses above) for the listing of books for sale.

Or write:
Milton Sherman Bookseller
P.O. Box 623
Armonk, NY 10504-0623

▲ FURNITURE

▲ ANTIQUES

Antiques at the Tollgate
1569 New Scotland Rd.
Slongerlands, NY 12159

Barretts Bottoms
Rt. 2, Box 231 Bower Rd.
Kearneysville, WV 25430
Catalog

Boston Road Antiques
498 Boston Rd.
Groton, MA 01450

Douglas H. Hamel Antiques
RFD #10, Box 100
Concord, NH 03301

Shaker Heritage Society Antiques Shows
Managed by Oliver & Gannon Associates
P.O. Box 131
Altamont, NY 12009

Willis Henry Auctions, Inc.
Annual Shaker Auctions
22 Main St.
Marshfield, MA 02050
Catalog of 360 lots sold at last auction

▲ REPRODUCTIONS

Dana Robes Wood Craftsmen
P.O. Box 707, Dept. SP
Lower Shaker Village
Enfield, NH 03748
Catalog of handcrafted new Shaker-style furniture

Great Meadows Joinery
Gene Cosloy
P.O. Box 392
Wayland, MA 01778

Joe W. Robson, Cabinetmaker
14 Prospect St.
Trumansburg, NY 14886

Shaker Legacy
SR 5 North
Shipshewana, IN 46565

Shaker Workshops
Box 1028-SS
Concord, MA 01742
Catalog of Shaker-style dining chairs, tables, beds, and clocks, available in kits or completely finished

The Workshops of David T. Smith
3600 Shawhan Rd.
Morrow, OH 45152
Catalog

Robert A. Wurster
Rt. 4, Box 9
Berkeley Springs, WV 25411

Yield House, Inc.
Rt. 16
North Conway, NH 03860

▲ REPRODUCTIONS, MASS MARKET

Lane's Shaker collection, available wherever Lane furniture is sold.

▲ MISCELLANEOUS

Connecticut Cane & Reed Co.
P.O. Box 762
Manchester, CT 06040
Basket molds and chair tapes

Kohl-Lection
2325 Anderson Rd.
Suite 105
Ft. Mitchell, KY 41017
Shaker "Tree of Life" chart and kit, and design samplers charted for counted cross stitch

Martha Wetherbee's Basket Shop
P.O. Box 35
Sanbornton, NH 03269
Shaker baskets, basket kits, and workshops

Quiltmakers-Depot St. Shop
SR 5 North
Shipshewana, IN 46565
New Shaker-style quilts, woven rugs, boxes, etc.

Sabbathday Lake Shaker Museum
RR1, Box 640
Poland Spring, ME 04274

Joel Seaman
Stoneykill Rd.
Canaan, NY 12029
Dovetailed Shaker carriers

The Shaker Seed Box Company
6656 Chestnut St., Old Town Center
Historic Mariemont
Cincinnati, OH 45227

Ann Black Sturm
c/o Thomas Black Jr.
1068 Parrish Rd.
Richmond, KY 40475
Shaker stereo tape cassette recorded at Pleasant Hill, KY, with accompanying songbook

John Wilson
500 E. Broadway
Charlotte, MI
Instructional video, directions, and workshops on oval-box making

▲ SHAKER MUSEUMS

Canterbury Shaker Village

Canterbury, NH 03224

Open May 8–October 21.

Closed Sunday and Monday.

Guided tours and craft demonstrations

Fruitlands Museum

Prospect Hill

Harvard, MA 01451

Open mid-May through mid-October, Tuesday

through Sunday and Monday holidays.

Tea room, shop, and nature trails

Hancock Shaker Village

P.O. Box 898

Pittsfield, MA 01202

Open daily, May 29–October 31; open April 1–

May 28 for daily guided tours of selected buildings.

Museum shop, lunch shop

Mount Lebanon Shaker Village

Box 628

New Lebanon, NY 12125

Open daily May 29–September 4; September 5–

October 31, open Friday, Saturday, and Sunday.

The Museum and Lower Shaker Museum

Box 25

Enfield, NH 03748

Open May 15–October 15, Monday through Sat-

urday; October 15–May 15, open Saturday and

Sunday.

Sabbathday Lake Shaker Museum

RR 1, Box 640

Poland Spring, ME 04274

Open Memorial Day through Columbus Day daily

except Sundays.

*Introductory and special tours, workshops covering

arts and crafts, summer concerts*

Shakertown

Shaker Museum

South Union, KY 42283

Open daily May 1–November 1.

*Ten-day annual Shaker festival, with craft demonstra-

tions, musical drama*

The Shaker Historical Museum

The Shaker Historical Society

16740 S. Park Blvd.

Shaker Heights, OH 44120

Open Tuesday through Sunday year-round.

Shaker furniture, antique exhibits, and lectures

The Shaker Museum

Old Chatham, NY 12136

Open May 1–October 31.

Room settings and displays

Shaker Heritage Society

Shaker Meeting House

Albany-Shaker Rd.

Albany, NY 12211

Open Monday through Friday.

*Tours, World People's Day featuring Shaker crafts

and food*

Shaker Village of Pleasant Hill
Shakertown at Pleasant Hill
3500 Lexington Rd.
Harrodsburg, KY 40330
Open daily, year-round.
Special programs, restaurant, inn

Museums to contact include:
Winterthur Museum and Gardens, Winterthur, DE
Metropolitan Museum of Art, New York, NY
Warren Country Historical Society, Lebanon, OH
Shelburne Museum, Shelburne, VT
The American Museum, Bath, England
Museum of American Folk Art, New York, NY

▲ SHAKER STUDY GROUPS

▲ NORTHEAST/NEW ENGLAND

Boston area:
Mr. Steve Paterwic
168 Quaker Rd.
Springfield, MA 01118

Rochester, New York area:
Ms. Fran Kramer
17 Golf Ave.
Pittsford, NY 14534

Western New York/Western Pennsylvania area:
Ms. Jean Middleton
P.O. Box 310A
Station Hill Rd.
Nicholson, PA 18446

▲ MIDWEST

Illinois area:
Mr. Bill Lucas
2107 W. Lunt
Chicago, IL 60640

Michigan area:
Ms. Darlene Kohrman
7622 Sandyridge
Portage, MI 49002

Ohio area:
Mr. Richard Spence
823 Yorkhaven Rd.
Cincinnati, OH 45240

Wisconsin area:
Ms. Rachel Thorson-Schmied
3728 Odana Rd.
Madison, WI 53711

▲ WEST

Southern California area:
Ms. Nancy Hillenburg
2219 Falmouth Ave.
Anaheim, CA 92801

INDEX